Learning to Lead

Bob Garratt is a company director, consultant and academic. He is chairman of Media Projects International in London and of Organization Development Limited in Hong Kong. He consults in director development and the development of strategic thinking in Europe, Asia, Australia, New Zealand and the USA. He is Visiting Fellow at the Management School of Imperial College, London University, an associate of the Judge Institute of Management, Cambridge University and immediate past chairman of the Association for Management Education and Development.

Other titles in the Successful Manager series:

Titles in the Successful Strategist series:

Bob Garratt

Learning to Lead

HarperCollins*Publishers*

HarperCollins*Publishers*
77–85 Fulham Palace Road,
Hammersmith, London W6 8JB

This paperback edition 1995
9 8 7 6 5 4 3 2 1

Previously published in paperback by Fontana 1991

First published in Great Britain by
Director Books 1990

ISBN 0 00 637722 X

Set in Palatino

Printed in Great Britain by
HarperCollinsManufacturing Glasgow

To the memory of David Steel —
a developer's developer

Contents

Contents

Preface

When I wrote *The Learning Organization*[1] in 1987 I said in passing that there was a movement in British management education which seemed to be emerging around the process, rather than the content, of managing. Notable advances were being made in terms of individual, team and organizational thinking, creativity, learning and strategy, little of which could be found in the normal management education syllabus. The traditional 'hard' areas that defined 'management' as essentially US and manufacturing-orientated over the last 30 years are now under question by these 'soft' area challengers from the United Kingdom.

At the time it seemed an interesting detour on the global managerial map. Now it is being taken much more seriously. A distinctive 'British school' is emerging which has focused on these 'soft' areas of management and has gone way beyond the US concern over 'uncertainty' and 'chaos'. This school has grasped the challenges of managing in turbulent times to create, through practice, new theories for the shape and processes of effective organizations, the roles of management in the twenty-first century and the qualities of thought, ideas and learning needed to lead such organizations and to work in them. It is concerned with the processes by which we organize, often backed with very high-tech high-touch computing to generate the information base characteristic of this approach. It values the ideas and possibilities that abound in the uncertainties of a changing external environment and values the people, the only learning resource, of their organization. In essence it is concerned with both the process and the content of organizational learning – what we learn and how we learn it in our working lives. It is therefore a long way from the functional fixation and analysis-paralysis of the 1960s and 1970s. Learning at the rate of change is its core. Thoughtful action and authentic information are its bywords.

It is significant that the members of the nascent British School derive mainly from practice and empiric research by consultants and line managers. Whilst some individual academics have helped greatly, few of their institutions have – these have yet to go through the change from 'old order organizations' to 'new order organizations' and the subsequent learning process which many businesses, governmental agencies, nationalized industries, social agencies and consultancies have already experienced. Paradoxically, they have yet to learn how to become *learning organizations* in their own right. That process is only just beginning.

My own work in this area derives originally from that of the design theorists and practitioners of the 1960s and 1970s underpinned, as I moved into the field of management development, by such luminaries as Reg Revans on action learning; Charles Handy on organizational theory and structure; John Morris on the anthropological processes of management; Tom Lupton on his gritty approach to management and the social sciences; and Stafford Beer on cybernetics. Over time an Australian perspective was gained from Alistair Mant and Denis Pym together with a US perspective from Roger Harrison and the change work of Watzlawick, Weakland and Fisch.

My current work derived a lot of its clout from the work David Steel and I did at Dunlop Truck Tyre and Marconi Underwater Systems – hence the dedication. I am delighted to be developing my ideas and practice in happy coincidence with the new work on thinking by Jerry Rhodes and Sue Thame, and Tony Buzan; on strategy and creating strategic vision by Tony Hodgson, and Gunnar Walstam; on the learning organization by John Burgoyne, Tom Boydell, Mike Pedler and Ian Cunningham; on development by Ronnie Lessem and

John Morris; on the codification and diffusion of learning by Max Boisot; on creativity by Tudor Rickards; and on the future of organizations by Charles Handy.

It is an exciting time to be developing new theories and processes of management in the United Kingdom as the conditions are right for experiment and the development of good practice. The likelihood of serendipitous connections is high on such a vibrant network. This is only possible through the risk-taking and wisdom of those organizations that have urged us onwards. Thus I should like to thank in particular Barry Welch of the TSB Group, Mike Bett of British Telecom UK Communications, Janice Caplan at Midland Montagu, John Shrigley at GEC–Marconi Group and Dave Wilkinson at Bradford Metropolitan Borough Council for their encouragement in the United Kingdom. In Hong Kong, Peter Barrett and Anthony Griffiths at Organizational Systems Ltd, John McGuigan at Baker & McKenzie, C. H. Tung at Orient Overseas and Hai Chi-Yeut at Hutchison International Terminals have all been willing to experiment and encourage. So too have our colleagues in the classes and factories of the China–EEC Management Programme in Beijing. I pray that they and their organizations survive and flourish to show just how important learning organizations will be in creating modern China.

This last thought is true for any country in this increasingly inter-related world and has been the spur to writing this book.

Last but by no means least I should like to thank Mike Fishwick of Fontana Paperbacks for his kindness in letting me adapt parts of *The Learning Organization* for the first and last sections.

Bob Garratt
Villa Gabrielle
Tourettes-sur-Loup
France

Introduction

Learning is central to the survival and growth of all organizations. This fact is only just being appreciated as we begin the design and managerial processes of our twenty-first-century organizations. Many of our current leaders have received little training for their present job of directing their organizations. They will need to be trained and developed for the challenges of the new century. When we combine the need for learning and the need to develop directing ability we create the idea of the *learning leader*.

Can learning leaders be developed and is there a real need for them?

One has only to cast one's mind back to no more than three or four national disasters to see the need. Public enquiries on tragedies sadly produce mountains of evidence of the lack of learning systems in organizations. Recent tragedies such as the sinking of the *Herald of Free Enterprise*, the Kings Cross underground fire, the Clapham Junction rail crash and the Hillsborough football stadium crush were all the more poignant as the evidence produced showed that the knowledge necessary to help avoid the disaster already lay within the organization. The problem seems to have been the lack of a system of learning to allow information to flow to that part of the organization charged with responsibility for taking preventative action. Most importantly, there also seemed to be no organizational climate where knowledge could be passed and received freely and openly in the interests of the organization and its customers.

This is common to many organizations. The lack of a learning system, by which they can become both more effective and more efficient, often leads to a climate where withholding of information, malicious obedience to patently stupid instructions, a habit of buck-passing and risk-avoidance – characterized as 'Oh! I thought they were doing that' – all combine with each other to destroy co-operation. When there is added to this an unwillingness to show moral courage by the leaders of teams and organizations, then the conditions are right for the creation of a non-learning organization and ultimate corporate collapse.

In the United Kingdom this point is now sharpened as both company law tightens on the liability of directors and directors are under threat of being charged with corporate manslaughter in extreme cases. Paradoxically, top managers now mouth the words 'our people are our major asset' but do not behave as if this is so. Yet it is only the people comprising the organization who are capable of learning. So how can we lead them and organize ourselves to learn continuously and reduce the chance of making a mess in future?

Rather than rush into visions of a brave new world it can be helpful to look at the pain of the present and the lessons of the past to help deduce solutions. Corporate failure is a fruitful area of study.

The death of a non-learning organization is often a slow and grizzly business. Shareholders, especially institutional investors, are rarely willing to intervene directly in corporate affairs by asking wise questions about an organization's effectiveness and efficiency. They prefer to vote with their feet, as do many of the good staff. Those remaining have to cope as best they can. The bright and the quick, having moved out first, are followed by successive waves of leavers. These are the very people the organization can least afford to lose, as it becomes less able to cope with change. This would not be too bad if the external environment – the political, social, economic, technological and physical contexts – were stable.

It patently is not, nor can anyone predict a time when it might be so within our lifetime. So when a non-learning organization meets a turbulent external environment the question is not whether it will survive, but rather how long will it stay afloat? The period that corporate bankers and shareholders are willing to keep such an organization liquid seems to be shortening. Remedial managerial action during this period increasingly resembles the proverbial process of rearranging the deckchairs on the *Titanic*. Eventually a financier will declare that the organization has been brain dead for years and switch off the financial life-support machines to a strange blend of sadness and relief all round.

Need it always be so? Certainly not. There are leaders, managers, staff and organizations who realize the simple ecological fact that for any organization to survive and have a chance of growing then its rate of learning has to be equal to, or greater than, the rate of change in its external environment. This is easy to say but difficult, though not impossible, to achieve.

To me the learning of the people who comprise an organization is critical in determining its survival or death. This sounds distinctly odd, even 'soft', to many leaders and managers. Surely, they say, businesses are about such 'hard' outputs as goods and services – iron, coal, cars, boats, banking, airlines, etc – rather than learning? Isn't the 'learning' approach another limp-wristed academic theory? No. Later in the book I look at the very hard core of this 'soft' approach, and argue that the learning of an organization will be its main tradable asset in the twenty-first century. It is already measurable; intellectual property rights are being established over this learning with court cases being fought over investment in learning and these rights will affect corporations for decades to come. How can leaders and managers afford not to be involved in such learning?

The simple answer is ignorance joined with the non-learning habits mentioned above. The problem is to get such people to see that the process of 'development' is crucial to their survival and that of their organization. All the learning invested and accumulated in many parts of their organization is of no use unless the people in the middle and at the top of that organization can value it and turn it into the good of the whole. They have the ability to control, often unknowingly, the climate for, and the flow of, learning in their organization. That they typically do not is only too easy to see in the majority of enterprises.

Why should this be so? In companies, and at conferences, I outline the argument above and usually get an enthusiastic response. Yet this is less often turned into behaviour in company. The intellectual and practical connections between individual and corporate brain, hands and heart seem loose. This is true in my experience of large numbers of European and Asian managers, and seems to be reflected in all national cultures. What is going on?

From my researches over the last 15 years with some 2,000 top managers I have noticed two key issues which seem to block the creation of the climate for a *learning organization*. Both are within the individuals who direct their organizations. The first is a lack of *strategic awareness* of their leadership role. By this I mean that they have rarely been through a rite of passage which says

> you are now so valuable to us that you must leave the day-to-day operations of the organization, and have time and space to think about how effective we are in relation to the changing world, what the future of those changes might mean, how we can position ourselves strategically and how we can create a system of rapid learning so that we may keep up with those changes.

The second is that even when this is said it is rarely delivered because no personal development process is in place to allow directors to learn how to do this. Neither is time or money budgeted to encourage directors to learn this new key role.

Consequently, those promoted often think that it is not 'legitimate' to develop themselves and they get hooked into their old *operational* level habits of firefighting the immediate rather than the strategically important. This action-fixated rather than action-learning approach is the curse of top management. I was naïve enough to think when I entered management education in 1965 that people were called 'director' because they gave direction to their organization. Whilst observation of directors' behaviour quickly disabused me of the validity of this idea, I still stand by it as a belief as to what directors should do – direct.

When I reached a position where I was asked to educate top managers on policy and strategy, I took a stance with my clients that this was not wise unless a simultaneous process of developing the personal qualities of these leaders was also agreed. Both are necessary, but neither is sufficient alone. Together they have a highly synergystic effect which can transform organizations through a series of interlocking developmental processes.

I use the word 'development' here rather than training, teaching or education. It is useful to define these terms as they are often part of the block in many leaders' and managers' minds. I am not focusing in this book on the training of directors and managers. 'Training' – the process of acquiring specific knowledge and skills needed for specific pieces of work – is necessary but not sufficient for what I mean by 'development'. Training can sound demeaning to some leaders even if they are the very ones who might need it most. It can sound too short, sharp and simplistic to others.

My focus is on development, by which I mean the process of revealing and bringing out what already exists within an individual, adding to it where appropriate by training and education, and then making the results manifest through their being seen to be used and to celebrate what is developed. For those fans of the film *The Producers* the end of a developmental stage is to feel happy with the idea of 'if you've got it, flaunt it!' But development, more than training and teaching, needs to be taken at the speed of the individual because it is a process of personal maturation. It cannot be rushed despite the many pressures to do so in modern organizations. On the other hand, once a person has learned how to learn regularly and rigorously then the return on the investment is lifelong, and both training and teaching become much easier, especially when the development process is backed by good coaching from the boss.

I am arguing that as development moves into the direction-giving levels and roles of an organization we need to assess what we have to offer directors in terms of acquiring the necessary thinking, knowledge, behaviours and skills for their new role. This is technically easy to do as Britain has the most diverse and tested range of management development processes anywhere in the world. But Britain has mainly class-room rather than real-time provision. Only when a proper assessment of directors' attitudes, knowledge and skill is made can one take a view as to what needs to be developed both for the individual and, more importantly, for the top team which he or she will be joining. The need for this real-time developmental process is the theme of this book.

'Education', like 'teaching', has become sadly demeaned in our society. For me it is the summation of those skills, atti-tudes, knowledge, behaviours, values and beliefs which transcend the individual subject inputs and create the well-rounded 'educated' individual – the person who has pushed to the limits their abilities in body, mind and spirit. Most modern education, and family life, misses this entirely and we are the poorer for it. We, therefore, have to do a lot of our 'education' inside our organizations and this is something for which few of us are equipped. However, I do see the new emphasis on learning processes to develop the body, mind and spirit of members of organizations as an indication of what life might be like in the twenty-first century.

This book is divided into five main chapters. Chapter 1 deals with the development of the individual director. It looks at why so few actually direct and shows ways in which they, and their fellows, can become comfortable in developing themselves and their organizations to give direction and leadership.

Chapter 2 deals with the development of others. If you are to create the climate of the learning organization, then it is necessary to coach, counsel and train others to do the same as you. This chapter looks at the systems, provision and techniques which can be applied in organizations to develop people for a range of flexible roles in organizations.

Chapter 3 deals with the development of our organizations. It looks at learning as a tradable asset, at learning as a capital investment, rather than an annual budgetary cost, and then looks at the developmental change process needed to achieve effectiveness.

Chapter 4 deals with creating the climate of the learning organization and the development of the processes for continuous organizational transformation.

Chapter 5 gives a very brief prediction of the future shape and processes of twenty-first-century organizations.

In the wider context I see this book as an interim report on the development of the new British School of management and would value any feedback from readers as we head into the challenges and turbulence of the twenty-first century.

Development and Directors

The Short-sighted Rhinoceros

> If I had known how little fun it would be as a director, I do not think that I would have accepted.

> My family were delighted, my friends were delighted if a little envious, and my staff thought that it was great that one of us had made it. The only problem was that after a few months I felt totally inadequate, became depressed, and dreamt only of getting out, or back to the security of my old job.

These two comments, the first from an international banker, the second from an engineering director of a major company, both of whom had 'made it' to general management level in their large companies, are typical of the comments I come across each day in my professional life. What is this curious paradox, that at the very moment of apparent career success things seem to start going wrong, often irretrievably? Does the Peter Principle[2] hold good? Are people always promoted to their level of incompetence?

In my experience the majority of people called on to lead and direct their organizations think this is so – and they are unhappy about it. They feel cheated at the last hurdle. They may have the 7 series BMW, the stock options, cheap loans, service contracts, golden parachutes, performance-related pay and all the paraphernalia of modern corporate 'reward packages'. Yet they do not feel fulfilled because they know that they are not doing their job as well as they could. On the other hand, they say that it is often very difficult to know what the directing role entails, and there is usually little if any help to get into that role.

Why should this be? I suspect that it is because of the way we design our organizations, and the way we handle power within them. When I became interested in this area in the mid-1970s I found little to help me. By the early 1980s various pieces of work were published which reflected on organizational structure and leadership and followership styles. Professor Gordon Redding[3] of Hong Kong University produced a short comparative study of US-, UK-, and Chinese-owned and run companies in Hong Kong. He looked at three hierarchical levels – top managers, middle managers and the workforce. He demonstrated in graphic form that each had distinct characteristics.

The Chinese companies were entirely dependent on the leader, significantly referred to as 'the big man', who determined from day to day what they would do, how they would do it and who would do it. They were responsive, flexible and fast moving but also seen as chaotic at any given point in time. The structure, values and direction were all held in the head of one person. To the outsider unless you knew the big man and how he thought then the whole seemed often anarchic as departments and individuals tried to second guess what the leader might want. The organization was highly personal, even feudal in style, and its view of its mission and relationships was defined personally rather than in relation to the good of the impersonal whole.

The US-run companies were relatively impersonal and well-ordered in their style at the top and middle levels with good systems, clear lines of authority and tight performance measures. However, when these systems met the local workforce there was a great deal of conflict and misunderstanding which dented both their effectiveness and their efficiency.

The British-run companies showed an organization of apparent anarchy at both the top and the bottom of the organization held together, and apart, by a thin film of middle managers who had control by creating barriers through which messages could pass from top to bottom, or vice versa, only via them. They had a picture of the good of the whole which was never made explicit outside their immediate circle but which allowed them to operate effectively despite great odds.

This British example interested me for two reasons. First, because it was so true of many companies that I knew back home where the top people did not act as a strategic team but rather as a bunch of individuals loosely bound together by the central heating system; and where the undirected workforce found their own salvation for the most part. The middle managers fought an heroic but ultimately doomed battle on two fronts and became embittered or demoralized because they could never see the top and bottom seeking a common cause. This caused me to wonder who gave direction to such organizations. From prolonged observation it seemed later that no one did, but at least the middle managers managed to stop the worst excesses of the other parties.

The second reason for my interest flowed on from this. I am very aware of the implosion of middle managers. We are losing the comfortable fat middle of our organizations as a mixture of cost cutting, information technology substitution and old age do their work. If British organizations lost this stabilizing factor of middle managers and the top and bottom had to face each other, we would have a heady, if unstable, situation. Many argue that this is precisely what is happening in our organizations and I shall go into this in greater depth in Chapters 3 and 4.

Why should the role of directors in this 'new order' be developed? Suffice it to say here that the forces for doing away with 'the fat middle' are now so strong that we must do something to show leadership and direction both within the top managers of an organization and between them and their workforce.

Some cynics say that such anarchy in our organizations is the normal situation and there is little that can be done about it. I think that our organizations are much too important to our society for them to be blundering about like short-sighted rhinoceroses – the physical, social, economic and political impacts can be too serious. So I have been looking for ways of describing the necessary roles and skills, particularly at the top of organizations. I have been very keen to find processes where the people charged with giving direction to their organizations could learn how to do so. How does a senior single functional manager become a *learning leader*?

What follows in this chapter could be seen as very depressing and negative. In one sense it is, as my work in many countries has thrown up the same sorts of problems for directors trying to become competent. The good news is that whilst this has been a hidden problem for many years there is now a noticeable move to talk about the issues and to do something about them. Chapters 2 and 3 show the positive responses to the negative issues of Chapter 1.

The Basic Development Process – and Where It Goes Wrong for Directors

In the end a key clue came only on going back to fundamentals. I reviewed what was known of the basic process of people maturing in their jobs. This has been well known, if little used, for years. There is a six-part process[4] which describes on the one axis the maturity achieved in a job, and on the other the time elapsed (Figure 1.1).

The Process of Developing Maturity in a Job

Let us go into more depth with this model; it is central to the argument for development at all levels of an organization. The first stage is 'induction'. This is often handled well in organizations. It involves the introduction of newcomers to their workplace, their workmates, the work itself and the organizational culture. Usually someone, a colleague or a

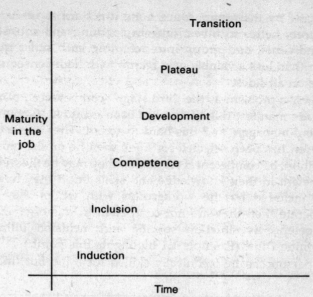

Figure 1.1　The basic process of development

supervisor, is detailed to keep a watchful eye over new people and induct them into the job and the culture – the way we do things around here.

'Inclusion' is the second stage needed to mature in a job. This is an altogether more subtle concept and is rarely managed well by either the individual or the boss. It is about being accepted by your workmates – and holds good at any level of the organization, including directors. This is not so much about your technical abilities, for which you were presumably selected for the job, but more about your personality and behaviour, and whether they will fit with those that already exist in the workgroup. People are rarely selected on such criteria. Yet these latter elements are the things on which you will be included, or excluded, from workgroups. Management of the inclusion process in the early stages is critical as the decision to accept or reject someone is often taken rapidly and implicitly by the group. Once done it is hard to undo. It is, therefore, better to invest time in coaching and counselling the individual and group into accepting each other quickly rather than lose a valuble new recruit with high consequential losses on all sides.

This is a problem as the third stage, 'competence', can only be made manifest fully if one has been included. Some directors and managers find this hard to accept. They argue that if a person has been selected for a job then he or she must, by definition, be competent. I argue that they may be theoretically competent in their knowledge and skills but if they have not been included by the workgroups with whom they must co-operate then they are not competent in this organization. Competence is situation specific and inclusion ultimately determines this. (Example 1.1 highlights this point.)

A person can be technically skilled for a job but find that

Example 1.1

A personnel manager was sent to the west coast of Scotland. She was new to the company and had many things going against her for inclusion – she was English, young, female and had come to regrade the working men's jobs. The first weeks were slow and painful with the lack of inclusion being made apparent each night as she sat alone in her hotel, despite having made attempts to join in the lively social round. One night during the third week a number of the men came to her hotel for a drink and found her there. They invited her to a drink and gave her a local whisky. West coast malt whiskies are relatively unknown and an acquired taste. To their surprise she named it immediately. They lined up more. She did not drink them all but named each one. Nothing much more was said that night but next morning when she went on site the message had gone before her – she was all right and could be trusted to look after the participants' interests. The job went ahead rapidly and well. The message also travelled quickly back to her headquarters base. The 'handling' of the Scots was much admired and led to her rapid acceptance as a competent team member back home.

he or she is seen as highly competent in one organization and a disaster in another.

Some of the saddest people I meet in organizations are those recruited for their undoubted expertise but who never became included. They roam the organization like the Ancient Mariner seeking someone to tell their story to and thereupon 'he holds them with his glittering eye'. This definition of the organizational bore belies a tragic piece of abuse of scarce human assets. I have noticed that the syndrome is particularly pronounced at the top of organizations where someone has been brought in from a very different culture and is left to sink or swim because 'it's all right, the others will accept him because he's so good in his own field'. This prejudges their ability to be accepted and valued by the different workgroups. This has also a major effect on organizational 'culture', with which I shall deal in Chapter 3.

The fourth stage of maturing in a job is that of 'development'. Once someone has been inducted, included and has demonstrated over time that they are competent in this culture then the social processes of the organization allow, and creative companies encourage, development – the bringing out of what is within the individual and making it manifest so that all may benefit. This is often felt to be so alien to people's expectations of organizational life that it must be made 'legitimate' before one can do it. This is a devastating comment on the alienating effects of organizational life, but it does seem true that one has to earn one's competency spurs before one can go through the rite of passage into becoming a recognized personality in the organization. Again, this seems especially true of directors. The problem is often to find the rite of passage. Sometimes it is to be seen as being included through being invited to stay for the weekend with the Chairman, invited to join an exclusive club to which the others already belong, asked to join a racing or shooting syndicate, or given a corporate season ticket to the director's box at

Arsenal fooball club. I have worked with clients who have been offered every one of these over the last year.

Once that part is over then the developmental process can begin in earnest. You are acknowledged, at any level of the organization, to be the sort of person that the organization wishes both to value, and to help grow its culture – its unique way of doing things. Then resources in the shape of time and money budgets are made available to you and the whole world of *personal development agreements* opens up to you – the explicit development contract between you and the organization. Chapter 2 looks at the technical aspects behind this idea, so I will not labour it here.

What I will stress here is that the developmental process operating at this fourth level of maturity helps a person move from just having a 'job' in the organization to having a 'role'.[5] A job is specified through the job description. When a personality and set of competences are attached to that job and developed, then an organizational 'role' is created. For example, a person can do a job competently but not feel completely fulfilled by it. They can through a process of self-development of, say, new skills and attitudes expand their abilities and the job. By so doing they set themselves new challenges and targets which they strive to achieve. This is personally exciting but often organizationally difficult. They may well have taken over a part of someone else's job which was either not done well or not done at all. As time moves on and other such changes reinforce their competences in these aspects officially outside their job description the individual begins to develop a unique role in the organization and to be valued for it. The snag is then that it is often out of true with his or her formal job. This will play havoc with the personnel function's job descriptions and salary scales; but which is more important for the organization – written prescriptions or an energized person? Many organizations are beginning to lean towards the latter and that is when it is important to try and get the best of both through an integrated system of development. This is dealt with in detail in Chapter 3. The important thing to stress here is the attitudinal change from the twentieth-century notion of fitting fixed jobs to malleable people to the twenty-first-century idea of fitting the scarce people to malleable jobs.

The other two stages of job maturity need not detain us long here. They will appear later as re-energizing the 'blocked' manager (pp. 19–22) and in the Culture and Change section (pp. 98–100). The fifth stage is that of 'plateau'. This describes the position reached when there is no internal or external perception of development needed, competence is high, and the individual, their boss and staff are happy with things as they are. In a turbulent society this idyllic stage rarely lasts long. Because of our demography we have had a majority of directors and managers 'plateaued' for the last 15 years but that is now ending and working people are likely to have a more interesting time from now on.

The sixth stage of job maturity is that of 'transition'. If the model represents a total career then this would be retirement, or in the case of 25 per cent of British managers, death in service. If this is seen as a career stage then we are looking at promotion, redundancy, sacking, job rotation, headhunting, etc.

Whilst for the last two decades a lot of managerial focus has been on the latter stages of plateaued and transitional managers, because of the demography of Europe we are now seeing a swing back to the early stages, with a particular concern for retaining competent people at all levels. This is where development and personal development contracts can prove so helpful. Unfortunately, it is the directors themselves who often cause this not to happen.

The Problem with Directors is that they Block Things

Directors seem to assume that the basic development model holds good at all levels of an organization except the top. In theory it is as applicable at the top as anywhere; in practice it is rarely applied there. In all my experience across the world I have only come across one company using the notion systematically from top to bottom, and then it was applied rather mechanically. Why should this be so? Who *is* responsible for the development of directors? (See Example 1.2 on the present situation.)

It is rarely acknowledged that once a person is promoted to the direction-giving level of an organization, they will need any development at all. Time and money budgets dedicated to training and development tend to cut out before the direction-giving level is reached. What a major paradox there is here – that at the time people make their biggest career change from a specialist job to general management, and have the biggest impact on their organization if they do not perform well, they are given the least support! Organizational leaders, chairmen and managing directors seem blind on this issue and assume that the very act of promoting a person to be a 'director' will ensure that person becoming suddenly, miraculously, omnipotent. Whereas before they had been essentially convergent in their specialist thinking style there is now an expectation that they are all-knowing, all-seeing and have a highly developed sense of precognition.

The irony is that these people have typically spent some 20 to 30 years of their career following their highly specialist route to the top of the organization. They rose because of their specialization. Then they get a shock when they are expected to behave as generalists – looking across the organization and outwards to the complexities of the external environment, and taking a wise view of the benefits for the organization as a whole of different courses of action. This 'holistic' view of the director's role is becoming increasingly accepted as essential for the continued health and survival of organizations. However, if the developmental processes are not in place to allow people time to get into this holistic directing role then their behaviour can be bizarre at times.

When I work with directors on their development I find that

Example 1.2 Who is responsible for director development?
When asked who is responsible for director development there are remarkably consistent replies:

- **Shareholders** *either see themselves as too fragmented and out of touch to be able, or willing, to influence matters or, if institutional investors, say that their power is only to comment on overall rather than individual performance – and to express this through buying or selling the shares.*

- **Non-executive directors** *usually see themselves as too isolated and powerless to make constructively critical comments on the individual and group performance of boards. Only in the more far-sighted companies is this seen as a useful aspect of their role.*

- **Chairman** *often feels that this is beyond his/her remit as it should logically fall within the remit of the chief executive. The chairman will, though, sometimes accept a personal counselling or mentoring role.*

- **Chief executives** *often accept that they should do more to develop their colleagues but cannot see how to find the time or resources, particularly when pressed for short-term profits. Many neither understand nor value the developmental process sufficiently to invest in it. Moreover, there are power aspects to this approach. Having isolated 'directionless' directors failing to fulfil their organizational role means that a chief executive has more chance of maintaining one-man rule at the board. In such a case individual, or top team, development is very unwelcome.*

- **Executive directors** *are often the directionless ones. With all the other persons involved having little information about, or interest in, director development the truth is that the only people with an interest are the directors themselves. The snag is that they are often the last people in an organization to get the message about 'taking responsibility for your own development'. If they do, then they need to learn to combine to form a coalition of 'legitimate' self-developers.*

 If responsibility is not taken for self-development then the organization will simply have its top manager development done for it, and what is worse have no control over it. They will, like nearly half of the present British directors, fall to the blandishments of the headhunters!

typically over 95 per cent say that they had no system, nor encouragement, to develop their key role. This has been true of all cultures except the Japanese. So whilst they were delighted to accept the promotion they usually took a low profile in behavioural terms whilst they searched for what they were meant to do. There were rarely job specifications and few, if any, induction processes. The inclusion processes were non-existent. What looked from the outside like a 'top team' guiding the business was often reported to be in reality a fragmented group of individuals pursuing specialist, often selfish, goals without a common vision, an agreed direction or similar values.

So these new directors do what any anxious human being would do. They keep their head down, search for clues about what to do and how to do it, and begin to feel fairly wretched. It seems difficult to say to your boss or colleagues 'Look, I do not feel that I am becoming competent at directing – I feel I need some help and training.' Those few who ask can find it given, but some have also been demoted or sacked, so it is a risky tactic. They often find it difficult to talk to their partner about it, especially if the family is rejoicing in its new-found status and material benefits.

The Two Key Blocks for Directors

The crucial blockages occur in two ways. First, there are the nagging feelings and lack of knowledge as to what is competence at director level. I argue strongly that the majority of directors feel that they are not doing a competent job in giving direction to their organization. We will go into this in greater detail in Chapter 4.

Second, and following on from the feeling of a lack of competence, directors do what any human being does after a period of constant tension and uncertainty – they return to their position of comfort. To be precise, they do their old, specialist job again but this time do it unofficially. The relief is instantaneous as they slip back into the old well-worn routines, language and behaviour. The uncertainties which have existed since the promotion to director level fade away and life is distinctly more comfortable again.

The snag is that whilst they feel great others are now angry. The unofficial return to one's old job creates a blockage of development in the organization. The person most affected, and most resentful, is the one who was promoted to one's old job. They, quite naturally, take exception to their old boss coming back and sitting on their shoulders, thus blocking their development of competence in their new job. If this continues for any length of time then they will either leave to find a place which will allow them to develop properly elsewhere, or they will do the same as their errant boss and go back to do their old job. This knock-on effect continues down the organization and, in extreme cases, can lead to people admitting that they are paid one or two levels higher than the jobs they actually do. This is a sign of an unhealthy and unlearning organization.

The Role of the Top Team in Unblocking Organizational Learning

Having described the two key blockages caused by the lack of director development, the good news is that much successful work has been achieved in turning blockages into flows of learning. This starts from the recognition that the leadership and governance of an organization is the prime role of the directors as a group. Whilst this is assumed by company law it is often not observed in practice. Moreover, each director needs to be developed as an individual and celebrated for his or her unique contribution to the top team, before the flows of learning and information can energize the organization.

Five Conditions for Unblocking an Organization

The success my colleagues and I have had in companies has occurred when we have managed to create five specific conditions:

(i) A clear and unique *strategic and policy formulating* role for the top team. This is distinct from the usual run of board meetings about the governance of the organization. It excludes the day-to-day aspects of operational management.

(ii) Time and space for the top team to think and learn about their strategic role – linking the changing external environment to the dynamics of their internal organizational reality.

(iii) The creation of a true team at the top, valuing and using the individually developed strengths of each member through the careful assessment and development of these.

(iv) Delegation of problem-solving and puzzle-solving authority to those on the operational side, whose job it is to deal with the constant deviations from our plans and to bring the organization back on to its predetermined course.

(v) A willingness to accept that learning occurs continuously at all levels of an organization, so it is the responsibility of directors to create a climate in which it flows freely to where it is needed.

To an outsider such a list can sound naïve. Surely, they argue, that is what directors must do anyway? They should, but they often do not for the reasons outlined above. Being naïve in this area myself, although I hope intelligently so, I went back to the books and reviewed what was being taught about this area. I found remarkably little and what there was seemed to be contradictory. Business schools tend not to teach at the director level, but they do run short courses for them. Those

I looked at tended to be similar to their 'executive' offerings but with a different badge attached.

DEVELOPING A CLEAR POLICY AND STRATEGY ROLE FOR THE TOP TEAM

What struck me most was that what was offered had a core area which was small and almost exclusively analytical – concerned with the 'what' rather than the 'who', 'why' and 'how'. There was also little agreed language for the area. I had assumed that such fundamental concepts as 'policy' and 'strategy' had been well researched and agreed. But the texts seemed to be fighting about which was paramount – strategy or policy.

Having an interest in history and philology, I thought that this had been cleared up at least 3,000 years before by the Greeks, whose words we now use. Before that the Chinese had similar thoughts on the conduct of political and military affairs and had codified these through such books as *The Art of War*.[6] Their thoughts still hold good in less war-like environments.

●● Getting to grips with policy, strategy and tactics
'Policy' comes from the Greeks and entered the English language originally with a 't' in place of the 'c' – polity. It concerned and described the political external world of the organization. It is concerned with the dynamic, turbulent and uncertain world within which our organization exists and which shapes our ability to manoeuvre in response to such environmental changes. The ability to monitor and understand it is fundamental to our organizational survival. Yet it is rarely taken seriously at the top of an organization because it is 'difficult', 'diffuse' and 'soft'. So the focus is usually, and unwisely, downwards towards the day-to-day and tangible reality of the organization.

What policy is not concerned with, as it is in so many organizations, are such piffling aspects as the rules for car

15

parking space, holidays or payment for overnight stays. These may cause a great deal of organizational heat and little light but they are not 'policy'. I argue that true policy formulation is a key task of the direction-givers of an organization. It is they who define the policy, or political worlds, of their business so that others can plan the details of the ways in which the broad objectives may be achieved. This is what differentiates them as directors from the world of the goal-orientated managers and workers.

Strategy is where the broad political wishes begin to be made reality. This is where the broad brush deployment of resources is made. It is the world of the generals and their debates with the politicians. If the latter wish to invade, say, Thrace, then it is the generals who need to decide the feasibility of the whole and they decide which armies and navies, when, where and how. The word comes from the Greek via the French into English and means 'the command of a general, or generalship'. It is the art of projecting and directing the larger military movements and operations of a campaign – usually distinguished from tactics, which is 'the art of handling forces in battle, or in the immediate presence of the enemy'. Strategy is the key interface between political aspiration and organizational reality. It is a blend of the process of creative decision-taking and leadership, and rigorous analysis and reality-testing. As such strategy is a central and dynamic activity for directors and needs constant monitoring of the two environments between which it sits – the external and internal worlds of the organization. It is this facing two ways which creates many of the problems for directors and is why they often resolve this by taking the comfortable route of facing inwards only and hoping that the outside world will stay the same.

Tactics, nowadays usually called operations, deals with the day-to-day reality of reaching specific ends to ensure the achievement of the whole. It was the area of concern of the colonels. This is where now the broad deployment of resources is made reality. Goods are made, telephones answered, accounts written and the customer satisfied or upset. The colonel deploys a series of officers (middle managers) to divide the work into manageable units and they, in turn, divide the units down into the workgroups overseen by a first-line manager. This is where the detailed learning of an organization is done. It is here that the ultimate safety and survival of an organization is determined. I mentioned in the Introduction that many organizations do not appreciate this and do not set up systems to learn from the reality of customer needs and the efficacy of their existing organizational systems.

It has been a piece of folklore that the strength of the British army is its sergeants. They are reputed to be able to motivate their people and help in their survival despite the sometimes fatuous orders from above. I have noticed since 1986 and the refocusing on the importance of customer service and *total quality management* that there has been a major reconsideration of the whole operational area. Two distinct trends are now seen, which I shall review in Chapter 3 in detail. Here I shall just mention that the pressures of cost, closeness to the customer and investment in information technology have all combined to reduce the number of middle managers. This has both positive and negative effects. The positive ones are first to reduce the ability for different hierarchical levels to distort information and therefore learning up and down the organization. The second is the conscious pushing of delegated authority down the organization towards the customer-facing staff and the consequent re-establishment of first-line managers – the supervisors with real discretionary decision-making ability. The sergeants of old are becoming the customer-friendly supervisors of today.

This ancient hierarchy of policy, strategy and operations has helped the directors with whom I have worked to understand better their role and its ancient pedigree. It seems just as applicable to twenty-first-century organizations as to the ancient. Even the military analogy has not changed much.

Now we have 'markets', 'segments' and 'niches' but we will reach them through 'competitive edges', 'conquering the opposition', 'surrounding and defeating the enemy', etc. The ancients were sometimes a little wiser than some modern strategists who seem to think mainly in binary terms – win or lose, good or bad, them or us. *The Art of War* warns, for example, not to surround an enemy on all sides – three is sufficient so that there is a chance of honourable retreat and you do not expose your forces to undue risk. You win by conserving your energies and having an enemy you may some day need as an ally.

The old generals are now the chairmen dealing with the local, national and international politicians. The colonels are the chief executives and managing directors balancing the external and internal worlds of their organizations and delegating power down to the customer-facing staff who test the immediate reality of their organization. My concern in unblocking directors is to ensure that they spend a significant amount of their individual and collective time at the interface of policy and strategy. This can be hard at first on a specialist who is a director in name only. But it is that for which they are paid. How can we help such people get into role?

CREATING TIME AND SPACE FOR THE TOP TEAM TO THINK

I have already mentioned the need to create space for directors to get above the governance role of their organization and create time to think strategically about the future and the positioning of their organization for it. This is usually greeted with scorn when first suggested. People find it hard to treat it as a legitimate use of their already busy time, even though they 'know' that this should be an important part of their job. They realize that their behaviour belies the importance of the role. How can something be done about it?

●● Five keys to director skills development

Directing in an uncertain environment is an uncomfortable activity. There are five aspects of directing which help differentiate direction-giving from the other managing and administering roles. None of them is found in the normal management texts and all of them are essential to survival into the twenty-first century:

(i) Thinking and Reflecting. This is the main activity of a direction-giver as he or she integrates past roots, present reality and future possibilities. Managers are typically action-fixated after 20 or 30 years in the hands-on, day-to-day, operations cycle. To be expected to stop and focus on thinking as a priority can be quite unnerving. This needs time to develop in a person and is rarely available unless a time budget is consciously created. Even then the ability to think effectively on strategic issues is not widely developed. I will say more about this later.

(ii) Designing the Future. The essence of direction-giving is about creating or taking future opportunities. Sadly, many people who become directors are firmly rooted in past prejudices about how to manage or mimic the actions of other successful managers. This tends to make them over-judgemental of new ideas or trends and often forces them to see things in black and white only – good or bad, right or wrong – rather than in the more design-orientated mode of 'both . . . and', which is a much richer concept. That something can have aspects of both right and wrong in it allows for a range of possibilities about ways forward. This takes some learning.

Research shows that many managers are not that comfortable with dealing with present reality. They find reality-testing a problem and often have neither the systems nor the inclination to do it. They tend, therefore, to move forward in a world of fuzzy co-ordinates and

19

hope that nothing untoward will highlight the paucity of their information base. Typically, they have a good ability to sense what is occurring but do not have the hard data to back it. Knowing where you are is the key to being orientated and, therefore, able to give direction. This is another developable aspect of becoming a director although there is a very human issue of not wanting to see the full picture as it confuses more than it helps. A positive approach to this is also developable.

The same research shows that top managers can develop, and subscribe to, a strategic vision of where they wish to be. They have the capacity but do not always use it. This, too, is developable and relatively easy to achieve. What is more of a problem seems to be finding the way to get there. Director-level managers seem short on ingenuity. They are, therefore, less inclined to create their own future and seem to prefer to take what fate sends them. This ability to create and ingeniously deliver their version of the future is a crucial and developable skill for directors.

(iii) Seeing the Organization as a Whole. This is a particularly painful aspect for those directors who have come up the specialist route. Their investment has been in projecting their specialist discipline's superiority. To be asked to drop this habit and behave in a way that allows the total picture to be appreciated before a decision is taken on the organization's behalf is difficult and takes time to learn. This is a developable aspect of being a director but, as I shall argue later, can only be effective if the whole top team undertakes it as a joint development activity and budgets time for it.

(iv) Managing in Times of Turbulence and Uncertainty. This is an aspect which, like having to make time to think, can cause anxiety in a new director. The joy of working in the operational cycle of a business is that one can take hands-on action to rectify a deviation from plan and see a result. The frustration of working at a strategic level is that you have to react to an environmental disruption – an oil-price rise or drop, a change of political party, a stock exchange crash, etc – without an immediate result. It requires a different set of attitudes and behaviours. It is primarily an intellectual process of trying both to design one's place in, and to react to, the changing environment. This interplay of opposing forces is never 'won', it is a continuous movement – and needs people who are willing to develop themselves to enjoy and cope with uncertainty so that they can give true strategic leadership.

(v) Willingness to Learn from Others. Most of all a director needs to learn that he or she is not the fount of all knowledge in the organization. If anything, they are the least likely to know most things as people have good reasons to hide information from them. The abilities to be humble and seek authentic information at all levels of the organization – to test reality – via discriminating questions and to create the environment for organizational learning are developable and, usually, needed desperately.

THE CREATION OF A TRUE TOP TEAM

During my years of in-company work and director interviews the number of boards or general management groups who agree that they are a true top team can be counted on the fingers of one hand. They use the term to describe themselves to others but do not recognize the reality of their behaviour in it. Rather they characterize themselves as a group of individuals operating in isolation, or fragmented units, who come together only at formal and, therefore, uncreative board meetings and committees. This sounds damning, and it is meant to be. For all the usual distance between academics and organizational directors one is reminded in their descriptions of their

21

'team' of the quote of the university faculty being 'a bunch of individuals loosely connected by the central heating system'.

I have some key questions that I use to test just how much of a direction-giving team I have when I am asked in to work with a client:

- What processes have you outside the formal meetings to talk about ideas, possibilities and the realities of the organization on a regular and rigorous basis?
- When do you indulge in freeform strategic visioning before getting down to plans and budgets?
- When do you assess and revalue your personal inputs to the board and create maps of the individual resources available between you?

There is usually an embarrassed silence, sometimes an angry denunciation of such soft notions, or most typically an admission that we seem to prefer in this organization painful isolation to supportive co-operation as our teamworking style.

This is curious as the only reason for organizations to exist is the idea that the sum of their outputs is greater than the sum of the individual inputs. The division of labour creates specialist functions which can refine their operations, and the sum of these energized outputs, created through the social process of co-operating, is then larger than those individual inputs – the 'synergy' argument. Synergy has had a bad press recently because it has been used so often to justify ever larger takeover bids in much the same way that 'economies of scale' were in the 1960s. Sadly there are few case studies to show that synergy was ever achieved, and a lot of evidence to show that demergers seem to release more profits.

But in team and organizational teams synergy can be highly beneficial. That is why I argue for it at the direction-giving level. If a group of diverse individuals – in functional discipline, age, background, experience, etc – can be welded into a complementary team then there is every chance that the organization can develop a leadership which can help it survive and grow. The team can form the very centre of the two cycles of learning in a business – the external policy-formulating cycle; and the internal operational cycle. By positioning itself at the junction of these two cycles it can create a truly strategic role for itself and become 'the business brain' constantly monitoring both cycles of learning, absorbing the information and reacting to it in a responsive manner. I shall deal with this in greater detail in Chapters 3 and 4.

My ideal top team would know and value each other's unique inputs and use them to help create strategic vision and wise leadership for their organization. This implies that it is legitimate and necessary to know what each person is capable of doing, not just in their specialist discipline but at the higher level of overseeing the total organization – and of doing this as an effective team. That is, celebrating and using each other's complementary strengths, accepting where there is overlap and openly coping with it, understanding where there are gaps and plugging those in ingenious ways, and generally enjoying working with a diverse group who will challenge and stretch you so that you must develop to keep up with each other. I see this as the core of the development process for directors if they are to fulfil their wise direction-giving role.

●● Director assessment

There are many routes available to create the information base of the capabilities and aspirations of each director and the top team as a whole. These range from deep personality profiles of the type preferred by Michael Edwards when he was running British Leyland, to survival training in the Scottish Highlands in midwinter. The essence is to get high-quality feedback on both the individuals and the top team so that they can plan their personal and team development paths. The content and process of such assessments is given in Example 1.3.

My preference is for behaviourally based psychometric tests. My assumption is that our personality is with us by the age of seven, as the Jesuits will have it, and it will take a conscious and sustained effort to change it, even if it is agreed that this

---

Example 1.3 Roles, acting and the real person

One of the criticisms raised immediately by many directors of such psychometric tests is that 'they do not show the real me'. Such doubts usually do not last long as they find the inventories both non-intimidating and even helpful. The results can be cross-checked against the folk who work with you, particularly if the tests are behavioural. I have only had one case where the results were not real for the person, even though they were seen as real by all his colleagues. The director was head of marketing for a major international corporation. As such he was seen as an extrovert personable lively character who added greatly to the energy of the company. He saw himself as the reverse. But he loved acting and his job was 'an act' in his terms. He loved getting up each morning and getting into his role. Then in the evenings he could get out of role having done a good job and relax by being his real self.

---

is necessary. Why put effort into changing personality which is so deep rooted when you can change behaviours more easily? Others see, and people react mainly to, behaviour rather than personality – so learning the skill of making behavioural adjustment to suit the circumstance is a much better investment for the director and leaves his or her deep personality undisturbed.

Similarly, if you prefer action-orientated assessment – outdoor activities – the amount of debriefing needed to make sense of what really happened to you whilst feeling terrified as you prepared to abseil off a 100-foot-high railway viaduct, or swing on a rope over the River Severn, is enormous and, sadly, in my experience rarely happens to the depth needed. So why invest time and money in it?

That is why I prefer mapping and testing the behaviour of directors. It is tangible, can be adjusted and developed by the individuals in real-time, and allows others in your team to help you develop it if asked. It gives an immediate tool in terms of information and action. As a baseline I typically use tests which allow us to investigate in individuals, and the team, the consequences of such aspects as:

- Leadership and development style
- Thinking intentions profile
- Learning style
- Strength deployment preferences
- Group role preferences
- Influencing style

These allow maps to be drawn both for the individual and, most importantly, for the team as a whole. Whilst there will never be a perfect team profile, it is highly enlightening for all concerned to see where problems might, and do, occur. Usually pronounced patterns of behaviours appear in any top team – say, a tendency to be very judgemental, devalue ideas and avoid ingenuity in their work, to be unwilling to delegate authority to subordinates, and to be blocking in their development of staff.

Taking a specific group of very senior executives, I have listed typical characteristics which come across time after time in the top teams with whom I am asked to work:

(i)   A tendency towards active experimentation rather than reflection in their learning style.[7]

(ii)   A tendency to being highly political with each other and to reject the nurturing side of their characters.

(iii)   A tendency to be highly shaping of others in meetings rather than chairing them in a neutral manner to the benefit of all (illustrated in Example 1.4).

(iv)   A tendency to belittle the importance of information in preference to their judgement and to be uncaring about the completion of work they have launched (see Example 1.5 for an instance of this).

(v)   A tendency to fixate on reward-and-punishment styles of influencing others rather than having a range of styles including creating a common vision.

The patterns must be seen in all concerned. They are not

Example 1.4

The board of one of the largest organizations in the United Kingdom found they had got themselves into a series of highly frustrating micro-political binds. This meant that whatever they tried to do there was always a majority ready with reasons why this should not be done. When asked to draw as a group what it felt like to be in their meetings they came up with a rowing eight and a cox. The difference from normal was that the eight all had megaphones and were shouting at the cox, who was rowing wildly. The laughter created released a lot of tension. From investigating their preferred roles in a team it was found that they all tried to 'shape' each other into accepting their predetermined solutions to each problem presented. Few of them had any interest in chairing meetings in the proper neutral manner. Having ascertained this it took little time before people chairing meetings did so in a more nurturing way, checking everyone's ideas, information and commitment. If a person in the chair needed to shape, then they learned to hand over the chair to someone else until they had finished airing their views and exercising their power. This has worked remarkably well despite a great deal of scepticism at the start.

Example 1.5 Senior policemen and hard facts

I worked with a large group of senior policemen on their preferred thinking styles using the thinking intentions profile. They had assumed that they would be firmly based in the 'hard' areas of thinking – logic, hard facts and ingenuity. To their surprise they came out very high on the 'soft' side – commitment and firmly held personal values, sensing information and visionary capacity. This did not mean that they could not do the 'hard' side, rather that they started on the soft side through their (past-orientated) experience and only later rationalized their thoughts into logic. Whilst this worked well on many investigations it raised a lot of questions amongst them as to how they handled information in their managerial systems.

---

the property of the chairman or chief executive although both of these need to participate if a team is to be formed and sustained. Such 'glasnost' in a top team is often welcome, after initial nervousness, as it opens up debates which have

long festered. These debates are very useful devices for including new members into a team, and introducing new people.
They demonstrate to everyone their unique contributions as
well as their, and the team's, development needs. Such
inclusion opens the way for the rapid development of competence in the direction-giving role and helps set the climate
at the top for the learning organization to be developed.

The key to using these behavioural maps is to ask these
simple questions of the group: 'How can we be more effective
in our direction-giving role when we have this mix of people
in the team?', 'What do we overdo, and what do we need to
complement our mix?' The idea of a balance of mixes, in
ecological terms of there being 'sufficient variety'[8] in the
system, is a useful one. Many top teams are recruited from
the same specialisms, the same background, the same sex,
the same business experience, the same age, etc. Studies of
company failures show that companies that crash have too
much of the same in their top managers. Specifically, they
have:

- one-man rule
- a non-participating board
- an unbalanced top team
- a lack of management depth
- a weak finance function
- a combined chairman and chief executive role.[9]

It is to combat this sort of problem that I find the development
of a true top team the best antidote. It reduces dramatically
the organizational climate in which accidents will happen.

DELEGATION OF PROBLEM-SOLVING AUTHORITY TO THE
OPERATIONS PEOPLE TO RUN DAY-TO-DAY AFFAIRS
This is often the most difficult piece of learning for the new
director. It is a key to becoming a learning leader. It is easy
to accept intellectually that their new role is about direction-
giving and designing the future for their organization. But
faced with the reality of letting go most of their investment in

their past career path and having to learn their new role, then their hands and their guts tend to react despite what their heads and their hearts tell them. This ultimate career change is painful and disconcerting. However, it is not necessary to make the change in one bound. Indeed, it is unwise to try to do so. Delegation – the devolving of your organizational authority to your staff – is a necessary and developable skill. It takes time and nurturing to do well and the payoffs are highly desirable. A staff that has been allowed to accept delegated responsibility is likely to be more open, responsive, loyal and creative than one that feels blocked, sullen and liable to malicious obedience. To achieve the former and avoid the latter delegation needs to be planned and then experimented with in small doses until all parties are reasonably happy.

Directors have two major fears about delegating. First, that they will lose control of something for which they will be held ultimately accountable. Second, that they will not have enough to do if they are successful at delegating, and will then be found out with terrible, but unspecified, consequences.

The first fear, of losing control of something for which they are held responsible, is also a definition of the top roles of any organization be it business, government or voluntary service. There is no way in which top managers can keep their hands on all their staff's operations all of the time. That is why we develop them to take responsibility for their own actions. This gives us a way of learning from them what actually occurs and for them to learn from us what needs to occur. This mutual support is the basis of the learning organization. People have a natural propensity to learn and contribute to their organization's work. They gain recognition from it, and it is recognition by others that all of us seek. (Example 1.6 demonstrates the problems of non-recognition.)

Sadly, the majority of directors with whom I have worked try to keep their hands firmly on their staff's work, thereby blocking their development by stopping their ability to learn from mistakes. By so doing the directors then stress them-

---

Example 1.6 The problems of negative recognition

A leading corporate banker was headhunted into a new bank as a director. He was technically excellent but 'not good with people'. In his previous technical job this was not too much of a problem. His new job demanded more co-operation with others, and a reliance on his small and highly efficient personal office who had been a team for some years. He chose not to recognize their worth and rarely spoke with them except to give instructions. He had a principle never to say 'Thank you' to a staff member because he thought that soft, and unnecessary as they were paid handsomely. He did not become included with them, or his new top team colleagues. The quality of his work was seen as poor. He took more control of the work of his personal team. They resented this as they had worked well before he came and he refused to accept this. He took more and more of their autonomy away and told them to do only what he specifically instructed. They attempted not to acknowledge him but this made him angry so they decided between them only to do precisely what he said. The quality of their output fell further and his colleagues began openly to question the wisdom of his appointment. He was taken aside by the chief executive and asked to teambuild his now openly rebellious personal office. He said that he could not see the sense of this and took to shouting at his staff, who paid no attention to him. After eighteen months he was back with the headhunter and has continued through a series of short-term and unsatisfactory jobs.

---

selves and so set up a vicious circle of control, demotivation and poorer quality work, which leads inevitably to more control, etc. It is the nature of directing that you accept responsibility for actions you have not directly overseen. The job of a top manager is to select and develop people they trust to do a quality job, and to coach them regularly to ensure that such quality is maintained. Coaching is not doing the job for the staff. In fact the modern school of sport coaching does not tell anyone anything during the coaching sessions, but helps the person being coached to develop their own feedback system through asking questions of what is happening in real-time.

Research work on delegation shows that there is a great

unwillingness in many managers to go over the cusp (see Figure 1.2)[10] of leadership style from the 'telling' and 'selling' modes to the 'participating' and 'delegating' modes. One needs to go through each stage to lead an effective team, so having a range of leadership styles is not sufficient in itself. One needs also to be aware that sensitivity to the maturity of the group and then applying the appropriate leadership style is essential for effectiveness. It is only when one has measured and developed one's leadership effectiveness, in relation to

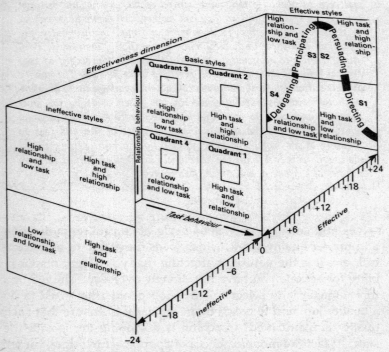

Figure 1.2 Leadership and development style

(**Source:** Paul Hersey and Kenneth H. Blanchard, *Management of Organizational Behaviour*, 5th edn, © 1988, p. 119. Adapted by permission of Prentice Hall, Inc.)

one's ability both to control and to delegate, that one is free to be able to find time to think and act strategically.

●● Strategic leadership

My response to the second fear about delegation, that 'I will then have nothing to do if I am successful at it', is 'Then you are not doing your strategic leadership job properly.' There are important things to be done at the strategic level and few of them are usually attempted. As examples I have listed below some of the major aspects of the strategic leadership job:

(i) Tracking major trends in the political, social, economic and technological environments.

(ii) Tracking what our customers need and what they think of us.

(iii) Tracking what our competitors are doing.

(iv) Ensuring that our environmental monitoring systems are effective for our needs.

(v) Ensuring that the management information systems are responsive enough to give integrative information for strategic monitoring and planning as well as operational data.

(vi) Travelling to see and hear what is happening in other industries and countries.

(vii) Creating the corporate culture we need to be effective.

(viii) Creating the climate and systems needed to ensure that the organization can learn continuously.

None of these, it will be noticed, is a particularly 'doing' type of job. These jobs are about investigating, thinking and planning, and lead on to coaching, influencing and counselling others both inside and outside the organization. They are about ensuring that you keep a viable and responsive organization capable of learning to survive and grow.

When I draw up such a list I am usually met by a chorus of

of course that is what the job should be. We would love to do that but around here if we are not seen to be busy and

> controlling all the time, then we are in trouble. We cannot
> afford to be seen to have a clear desk and be thinking, let alone
> be absent from it!

This is a useful point from which to explore the organizational
values of action-fixation (the curse of management) rather than
action-learning. Does having a clean desk and time to read
the newspapers before you start the work day make a less
effective director? Does having good time management and
personal effectiveness so that one can travel and think make
one a less effective member of a top team? Do we see ourselves
entirely at the beck and call of the chairman and chief executive, having to respond to him or her instantly as in the earlier
example of the Hong Kong Chinese company where all the
plans were held in the top man's head? If this latter is true,
why do we call ourselves a director? Are we not just a
manager-administrator?

A WILLINGNESS TO ACCEPT THAT THE LEARNING OCCURS CONTINUOUSLY AT ALL LEVELS OF AN ORGANIZATION AND NEEDS TO FLOW FREELY TO WHERE IT IS NEEDED

From the four conditions mentioned above it follows naturally
that the key facilitating role of directors is to create the climate
by which learning is encouraged, rewarded and allowed to
flow freely around the organization. If you can come to terms
with effective delegation, learn the skills of non-directive
coaching of staff, and know how to give recognition for quality
work and constructive criticism for bad work, then you are
well on the way to creating the learning organization. I shall
deal with this in much more detail in Chapter 4.

The good news about all five conditions for becoming learning leaders is that more and more organizations are beginning
to revalue the members of their board and create developmental processes through which they can become a truly strategic
top team. With this they have the basis for becoming learning
leaders of their organizations, and for energizing their staff to
take responsibility for their own problem-solving and, hence,

personal development. It is to the process and content of personal development in organizations which I now turn.

Developing Our People

The Present Context of Development – from Cussedness to Competence via a Great Lie

There is a law of human cussedness. It can be seen in the design of an ergonomically perfect chair when used by a human. No matter how good the design, our sensing mechanisms and need to explore and test our environment soon have us wriggling about, hanging legs over the edge, tilting it back as far as possible and generally treating it in a most unergonomic way. Similarly, in organizations there is a big difference between what they need and what they want. Michael Dixon of *The Financial Times* thinks that this is particularly true of the top managers, so much so that he posited it as one of his 'Laws of Organizational Stupidity'[11] – that the higher you rise in an organization the wider the divergence between needs and wants.

This is true of many of the organizations in which I have worked. But who assesses such top managers' needs? As I asked in Chapter 1 – who is responsible for director development? The only sensible answer is the directors themselves. It took me some time to realize that there is an inverse relationship between seniority and the level of input needed on many subjects. This is not to suggest that the higher you go the less skilled and more stupid you become. That is a well-honed organizational myth. I mean rather that the closer you get to the top then the less you need to know any subject in detail, but the more comfortable you need to be asking high-quality questions about anything.

Reg Revans has said that 'this is the point where you become less interested in knowing the right answers and more interested in finding what the right bloody questions are'.[12] It is one of the keys to directing that one can rise above the immediate puzzle-solving and 'programmed knowledge' and learn to ask 'discriminating questions' of others as a main activity – and feel comfortable about it. This use of discriminating questions to trigger others to do high-quality work rests on a paradox – the use of 'intelligent naïvety'. There is no way that a person trained, say, as an accountant can sit at a boardroom table and expect to ask detailed questions of, say, the personnel function. Many try, however, and reinforce thereby the internecine warfare found in too many boardrooms.

The point is that in accepting one's naïvety regarding a subject and combining it with one's native intelligence it is both possible and necessary to ask fundamental, intelligently naïve, questions about what is being proposed. The most powerful question is 'Why are we doing this?' but this is so powerful that it needs to be used sparingly to be effective, or it will lead to highly defensive posturing in others. But it does need to be used. The other 'able men and true' – what? when? how? which? where? who? – can be brought into play to have people explain to you, an intelligently naïve person in a position of power, what is occurring. From such explanations an overview – the 'helicopter view' – can be gained and an informed perspective taken on the wisdom of what is occurring in relation to the total organization. Feeling confident enough to ask 'Is this effective in helping us achieve our vision and objectives, or does it only suit a specific group's aims?' is a developable skill. It helps us understand the difference between 'cleverness' and 'wisdom' in organizations. There are many clever people about. Learning leaders need wisdom more than cleverness, and the ability to ask wise questions of others. This is in short supply, but it can be developed.

Why get worked up about intelligent naïvety? Because it is fundamental to creating the climate of the learning organization. But before we leap into that veritable jaccuzi of an idea let us stop and look at the way we handle our present ways of learning in an organization – training, education and development in all its forms: individual, team and organizational.

Learning in Organizations, and Great Lies of our Time

A fundamental point I wish to make is that 'learning' is not the province of the personnel function. Learning occurs naturally at all levels in a healthy organization and is the immediate responsibility of those to whom it happens. Organizational ownership of learning needs to be located within the line functions of an organization for it to be able to survive and grow. Learning is not the specialist property of service functions. Personnel functions may well act as postrooms for the organization of training courses, and the selection of appropriate developmental processes, but the learning, in terms of process and content, is much too important to be left entirely to them. The quality and transmission of the learning in an organization is ultimately the province of the line managers and the individuals themselves, led by the learning leaders – the direction-givers of the business. They alone can create the climate of the learning organization.

Our people are much too important to leave to the personnel function alone. In the days when people were treated as merely depersonalized units of labour such an approach may have been seen as acceptable, although unwise. Nowadays with the population profiles of the industrialized world taking a diamond rather than a pyramid shape – as a negative birthrate and a middle bulge move through each population – we see humans as an increasingly rare resource, a precious asset, who need including, nurturing and developing to keep them learning with you and for you as long as possible.

It is only too obvious that most organizations have not yet realized this and tend to mouth one of the great organizational lies of this world – 'our people are our greatest asset' – and then behave as if the reverse were true. The behaviour of the line managers and directors needs to be congruent with these words if one is to grow a learning workforce. This means building the development process into the day-to-day work. Just as directors need to transcend their daily existence to become more strategic so line managers need to be encouraged and rewarded for becoming real-time coaches and counsellors of their teams. It is a present trend that top managers are increasingly holding their line managers accountable for so doing – and developing new, integrative, measures through both the appraisal system and such indicators as labour turnover, sickness and staff development rates to ensure that they are on the ball.

The Changing Context

The UK context for management and organizational development has changed dramatically, and its position on the national political agenda has risen since the publication of two linked reports – one by Charles Handy[13] and the other by John Constable and Roger McCormick[14] – in 1987. They have raised a great deal of debate and have now led, through the Management Charter Initiative (MCI),[15] to a series of initiatives. Some have been dead ends, like the idea of management becoming a chartered profession. Others, like the Code of Conduct for Management Development (Example 2.1), and the Self Development Contract, seem to be on the road to being accepted nationally.

There is also a strong pointer to Government thinking on development processes. Whilst encouraging the positive aspects mentioned above they have also encouraged the more doubtful notion of developing a set of national competences for all managers and, by extension through parallel work in the National Council for Vocational Qualifications, for each job in the country.

Let us look first at the Code of Conduct and personal development agreement ideas.

Example 2.1 The MCI Code of Conduct

When your organization joins the MCI, it makes a pledge to both current and future managers through the 10-point Code of Practice.

Chief Executives will communicate and demonstrate to all managers their commitment to this Code. It is a formal recognition of the importance of management education and development. Your organization will promise:

(i) *To improve leadership and management skills throughout its structure.*

(ii) *To encourage managers continuously to develop their management and leadership skills.*

(iii) *To provide a coherent framework for self-development within the context of corporate goals.*

(iv) *To ensure that the development of managerial expertise is a continuous process, fully integrated with the work flow.*

(v) *To provide ready access to relevant learning and development opportunities – both internal and external – with requisite support and time released, appropriate to the organization.*

(vi) *To encourage and help managers acquire recognized relevant qualifications.*

(vii) *To participate actively in the appropriate MCI Networks.*

(viii) *Directly and through Networks, to strengthen links with management education sources, ensuring that the training offered will best complement management development programmes – matching corporate needs and future requirements.*

(ix) *To contribute to closer links with educational establishments.*

(x) *To appoint a director or equivalent to oversee the fulfilment of these undertakings; to review progress annually and, after evaluating the contribution to performance, set new targets for both the individuals and the organization; and to publicize highlights from the review and the new targets.*

CODE OF CONDUCT

Example 2.1 gives a watered down version of the initial draft. I recommend the earlier wording, given the likelihood of having to fight for staff in the future. This was that a company subscribing to the Code of Conduct would guarantee each of its managers a minimum of ten days' development each year in time and money terms, and would contract to this through the medium of a personal development agreement.

Some major companies are already subscribing to this notion, even after calculating the budgets, because they reckon that this will be one of the few tools they will have to keep talented staff in future.

PERSONAL DEVELOPMENT AGREEMENTS

The idea of personal development agreements is catching on fast. They are a contract between the individual and their organization which states that, for a given output of work, specified at least in volume and quality terms, and the achievement of mutually agreed targets of performance and behaviour, the organization will encourage through a regular appraisal the ability for the individual to develop themselves and, by extension, the organization.

Note that it is a *personal development* agreement, not a technical training one. It is about more than just getting the job done. It is also about helping the individual create their role in the organization via the *inclusion, competence and development* route. I have been involved in installing such systems in the financial services and electronic engineering industries. In every case we have found that there are four aspects of development which need addressing:
- Personal development
- Professional development
- Team development
- Organizational development

For each individual a time and money budget needs to be agreed. The details of all four aspects can be derived from a robust and regular appraisal system. This allows the individual and their line boss to link personal needs with corporate targets either directly or as a pay-off for achievements. The whole is designed to enhance the developmental cycles within an organization and, thereby, reinforce the climate of the learning organization.

The personal development aspect of the agreement is designed to cover a wide variety of issues – from learning a new language as a personal challenge, studying for a part-time degree, learning how to meditate, through to agreeing with the family a healthier regime for living and working. The essence of this aspect of development is personal challenge and personal growth. It is the aspect that is least influenced by organizational needs. It can also be the most unblocking aspect and help make achievements in the other three aspects more likely because of the energies it releases in an individual. It tends to be undervalued in most organizations but, with the change in demography, it is likely to have a lot more emphasis in future.

Such an approach can be dismissed as 'too soft' by many directors. It is wise to remember the derivation of the word 'management' in the English language. Coming originally from the Latin as 'by hand' it moves towards its modern meaning in Shakespearian times from the Italian 'maneggiare' – the breaking of horses. This macho notion of bringing wild things under one's control and imposing one's will is still a dominant style and is still a major mindset for the majority of managers. However, in the eighteenth century another root derived from the French 'menager' – a notion of good house-keeping and the domestic economy of a kitchen. This is a more nurturing view of management and one which is sadly underused by directors as many of my organizational climate surveys show. When I am talking of 'management development' I am thinking of a dynamic balance of both the achieving and the nurturing aspects of management. I argue that unless nurturing, and hence inclusion, is managed, then it is very difficult for people to achieve. In this sense personal development is a crucial, energizing force which opens up the rest of the development process.

I will deal with the ideas and processes behind *professional development*, *team development* and *organizational development* in detail later in this chapter, where I link them to the use of a robust *appraisal system* to refine constantly the full range of developmental needs.

Competences, Control and Professional Indemnity

The more debatable aspect of governmental, Training Agency[16] and MCI thinking is that it is possible to codify all managerial work in a national framework and then train managers to the necessary standard of competence, and assess them on it. Whilst a superficially attractive notion in terms of the transferability of standardly assessed competences, this assumes that people competent in one environment will be so in another. If you accept my argument that inclusion is the key to being seen as competent by the people with whom you work, then there is a potential contradiction between being assessed externally as competent and accepted internally as such. Experience in the professions that have tried such approaches for some time, for example architecture, has shown that this approach is of limited utility. They have achieved their 'professional practice' assessment through their own ends and without large sums of governmental, or semi-governmental, money being spent. Now we are faced with a massive governmental spend in this area, so one must ask – to what end?

I have no doubt that one can codify the knowledge, attitudes, skills and experiences which define the minimum competence level for any job – from grave digger to brain surgeon. That is the clever part. Whether it is wise to do so is a more important question. Why do we need it? Is not life now so dynamic that we will need continuously to recodify our competence specifications? What happens if this is not done fast enough for the real-world changes? Will we have a certification system, whether voluntary or compulsory, always lagging behind the competency codifiers? If we create a national databank of *vocational competences* on a voluntary basis, as at present, will there not be a temptation for a civil servant or politician to insist later on making it compulsory? If so, what will happen to organizational effectiveness? As the old Chinese curse says, 'May you live in interesting times.' In terms of development in the United Kingdom I think we have now entered those.

One of the few things that can be said in favour of the architects' approach is that if you can demonstrate that you are adopting a 'continuous professional development' approach, i.e. show that you regularly attend updating courses, then you can get a noticeable reduction on your professional indemnity insurance. This could have a significance for directors, managers and trainers, as the dreaded world of professional indemnity and 'due care' begins to rear its head in the courts, particularly in relation to the recent Companies Act tightening of directors' liability.

The Requirements for Successful Development
As I have mentioned, management development is on the national agenda for the first time in two decades via the Handy and Constable/McCormick reports and their follow-up through the curate's egg of the Management Charter Initiative.

Charles Handy's excellent report *The Making of Managers*[13] showed that on average British managers receive one day of training a year. As many big companies do a lot of training this means that most medium and small companies do nothing. All companies tend to get experienced people through recruitment rather than development. This has two consequences. It diminishes the perceived worth of existing staff in their own eyes when outsiders are regularly promoted over them and therefore de-energizes the very people in whom you have already made an investment. Separately, it helps line the pockets of the advertisers, recruitment consultants and head-hunters who make a killing from our inability to bring on our own people.

I am not arguing that we must only bring on our own staff, rather that it is unwise to assume that anyone working for you must, by definition, be unsuitable for development and promotion. This perverse piece of thinking has been prevalent in many of the clients with whom I have worked and seems to belong to the same school as Groucho Marx's 'I would not belong to any club that would have me as a member.'

What resources are available for us to use if we choose to counter this self-destructive and confidence-sapping thinking? The United Kingdom, curiously, has the most diverse and experimental management education and development provision in the world. Sadly, it is not a system. It has dozens of state- and privately run educational institutions, hundreds of training consultancies, thousands of self-employed trainers and developers and, just emerging, a few high-tech expert systems companies. In addition there is massive governmental intervention via the Training Agency. In addition the Department of Education and Science and the Department of Trade and Industry both make substantial contributions.

Despite all of these inputs not much seems to happen in terms of national organizational effectiveness and efficiency. I suspect that there are two good reasons for this. The first is that the directors of a company have not had much management education and development themselves and therefore do not know how to use those who have. In some cases they may even be perversely 'anti' those who have had. So there is a blockage at the top of many organizations to the effective usage of better-educated people. Second, there is no simple measure of the effect on national performance of education of all sorts. We are warned that the investment in education by, say, the Japanese and Germans will ensure that Britain is technologically, as well as verbally, illiterate to face the challenges of the twenty-first century. The weasel words about 'having to educate our children better' are mouthed by the politicians whilst they reduce, and fail to prioritize, the educational budgets they control.

When I surveyed the national scene for a Government agency I found to my horror that education was not a variable on any of the national economic planning models. It was treated, as happens in companies, not as an investment decision but as an annual budget item – trimmable to the whims and expedient decisions of chancellors. As there was no measure of the effect of national investment in education this was assumed to be acceptable, and the annual investment was made because it was a 'good thing'. How can one deal with such perverse thinking and behaviour at least in one's own organization if not at national level?

A System for the Mutual Development of People and Careers
The simple answer to how one deals with the investment, retention and development of one's staff, including oneself, is to have a robust system at all four levels – personal, professional, team and organizational – of development in your organization. Whilst this is often talked about, and sometimes budgeted for, directors and managers rarely behave as though they acknowledge and value its existence.

Using a basic model of a management career, the simplest statement of such a system would be a five-stage career development process (see Figure 2.1).

It is important to note that each stage has an assessment point through which one is measured, in a way appropriate to the organization (whether the measure is from the National Council for Vocational Qualifications (NCVQ) or self-derived), before managing the *induction* and *inclusion* processes. Each leads on to education, development and the acquisition of *competence* at the next level of one's career. Sadly, this happens rarely, mainly because we have not considered rigorously what it is we want from such a system. There is still a feeling that 'if we can afford a bit of training on someone's promotion

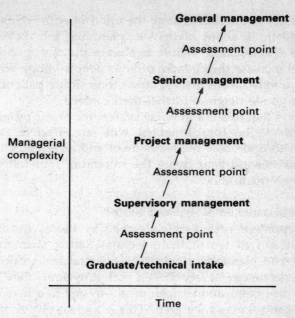

Figure 2.1 The career development process

then they should be grateful – because we did not get any'; rather than seeing it as a way of securing your investment in the scarce resource of people.

There are some deeper assumptions behind this simple model. First, that people have as great a say in their career as their bosses. This does not mean to imply that they can choose their jobs, but rather that the responsibility for putting themselves forward for assessment is theirs rather than just their line manager's. If they are found to be ready to progress, then they are helped to begin to prepare for that next step. If there is no higher job available to them, then they will be helped to broaden their experience whilst a suitable job is found within a guaranteed time. A personal development agreement contracts to bring them back to their upward career path at this specified time. The organizational issues this raises are manifest – but it does change the mindset with which bosses need to think about manpower planning, job rotation and people development. Failure to change the managerial mindset will increase the chances of your people voting with their feet in a tight labour market rather than sitting patiently waiting for you to deign to further their career.

I stress that this is a minimal system for career progression. It needs to be complemented with an effective appraisal system to undertake the assessment and development needs analysis necessary to create the minimum foundations of a learning organization.

The Performance-Based Appraisal System

Most appraisal systems are damned by those who use and suffer them as worse than useless. Rather than measure, debate and plan individual developmental and work targets, and generate useful feedback in both directions, they become either an organizational joke or a way for line managers to assert control over their staff. This is a great pity as performance-based appraisal systems are central to the success of any system of organizational learning. Bad mouthing of an appraisal system shows that it is badly designed. What constitutes good design?

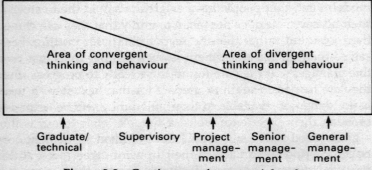

Figure 2.2 Continuum of managerial styles

In my experience effective appraisal systems have eight characteristics:

(i) They are the means of mutual discussion on past performance, present reality and future opportunities and targets.

(ii) They are related to measurable work performance and target setting.

(iii) They focus on observable behaviours, rather than speculate on fuzzy guesses of personal qualities.

(iv) They are directly related to the pay and rewards package of an individual.

(v) They draw out training and development needs, and contract to action on them.

(vi) They show the next possible career steps and why.

(vii) They give an overview of the likely ultimate career stage.

(viii) They have a fair appeal system.

I will go through these eight aspects in some detail as they are so important to help create the climate of learning and development at all levels of an organization.

Just before I do so I should point out that the essence of such a system is a person's performance in their job. This may sound trite but many systems I have seen have little about this in them, but a lot about the boss's personal views of the characteristics of the appraisee. This can lead to frustration and bitterness on the part of the appraisee, who often feels hard done by. In fact this is leading to some potential court cases about 'undue care' (professional liability) by bosses over their staff appraisals. We do not know the outcome of these but the fact that they are going to law at all should warn us of the need to design thoughtful and effective appraisal systems.

I ensure that the appraisal sheet is filled in in pencil by both the appraisee and the appraisor before they meet. At the meeting the aim of the discussion is then to reach a mutual scoring and a plan. To some directors this can sound most uncomfortable as they expect a confrontation because people will over-rate themselves. Experience shows that the vast majority of British appraisees filling in such a form underscore themselves and have to be coached into agreeing a higher score, rather than the reverse.

Taking each aspect in turn let us look in more detail at the components.

1. THE MUTUAL DISCUSSION OF PRESENT PERFORMANCE IN JOB, FUTURE POSSIBILITIES AND TARGETS

The most successful appraisal systems start with measurable performance indicators of past work. They state the targets, in both volume and quantity terms, budget performance, quality, resource usage, staff turnover, illness and satisfaction levels, etc, agreed at the previous appraisal and measure them against the present reality.

This forms the basis of the first part of the appraisal discussion.

2. THE RATING OF BEHAVIOURS

The rating of behaviours is fundamental to modern appraisal systems for two reasons.

First, behaviours are observable to everybody and can be easily checked out if there is a disagreement. This is the opposite of the old 'characteristics' approach which typically asked you to rate a person's, say, honesty on a 1 to 5 scale. This is a highly subjective judgement. As time went on and frustration built so did corruption of the system. One had such lunacies as a major national organization where the qualities approach generated such emotion that the management unions succeeded in getting an A (high) to E (low) scale changed because of 'unfairness' so that people could only be rated as B+ or B− or C+ or C−! Even then they wished to refine the system. On investigation it turned out that the emotionality was generated because people could not make an input to their qualities assessment and felt that the whole thing was too loose to be truthful, especially when it had such a direct effect on their salary and their career. It was, in fact, a good example of the organization being seen to exclude, rather than include, them.

Second, and very important for the learning organization, the choice of behaviours selected for assessment can directly influence the style and climate of the organization. Positive behaviours reinforced through regular coaching can, over time, affect attitudes, knowledge and skills, and ultimately culture – 'the webs of signification we spin for ourselves'. If you need a creative, responsive, customer-friendly, state-of-the-art, people-nurturing, networking type of organization, then the appropriate behaviours can be stated. If you need a calm, methodical, logical, judgemental, policing type of organization then those behaviours can be specified. It is in such specifications that the NCVQ notions of a national job specification are questionable. At present it does not allow for either the culture, or the stages of development, of an organization to be taken into account.

So behaviours like 'is seen to work well across departmental boundaries' or 'is seen to make effective use of his/her and other people's time' can be debated and scored.

To reinforce the culture notion it has been found particularly powerful to involve the people in the organization in helping to agree the behaviours for such a scheme. This has an energizing effect and ensures that they are committed to the appraisal process – people even become keen to be assessed.

●● Outputs from behavioural measures

The output from what are, typically, ten to twenty assessable behaviours needed for the corporate culture can be plotted individually for the personal rewards and collectively for feedback on trends in the organization. In this way the appraisal system becomes a part of the organizational learning. To ensure that line managers do not over-, or under-, rate their staff a normal distribution is often applied across the organization. As an example, it can be a rule that 60% of the population of every work unit will be accepted as performing adequately in their job: 15% will be viewed as doing slightly better and 15% slightly worse than the mean, and 5% as distinctly better or distinctly worse than the mean. Different organizations handle these percentages in different ways but the idea seems sensible and leads to little disagreement with those being assessed – provided only that it is seen to be applied fairly.

The companies which use such systems have found that such assessments are acceptable, if agreed mutually, for both pay rises and pay decreases. This latter case seems acceptable provided a self-development contract is entered into which guarantees the chance to reach the necessary performance within a given time and for which training will be guaranteed. This breaks an old adage of the personnel function – that appraisals and the salary interview should be handled at different times. Pay does not have to be agreed at the appraisal session but the basis of the next pay round will be agreed there. I realize that many personnel folk see this integrated approach as a cardinal sin – the problem for them is that it has worked successfully over a number of years in a wide range of companies and has had, to my surprise, the blessing of some trade unions.

3. FROM THESE MEASURES OF ACHIEVEMENTS AND BEHAVIOURS ONE CAN THEN CREATE A NATURAL INFORMATION FLOW INTO THE REST OF THE APPRAISAL SYSTEM AS FOLLOWS:

(i) New targets for the next period are agreed.
(ii) Training and development needs are identified which then form the contractual basis for the next personal development agreement, including time and money budgets and the dates by which the organization will

deliver such development. These will form part of the context of the next appraisal and are as much a comment on the boss's coaching and nurturing capabilities as those of the appraisee.

(iii) The next possible career steps are viewed in terms of the basic model of development shown in Chapter 1. The discussion is of the options and when they are likely to be available. These options will include whether to follow a specialist route or consciously to broaden one's experience, and the consequences of both. This needs careful explanation and thought and is, therefore, not a contractual element unless there is a special need for it to be so.

(iv) Similarly, the rather cruder view of the possible ultimate career stage needs be reviewed, but this is simply an indication and not a contract as there are too many imponderables. However, it does give the appraisee and the organization something at which to aim, and on which to take their own decisions about their commitment. In a time of growing labour shortage it helps concentrate the thoughts of top management on how to keep their people through offering rich and demanding jobs.

(v) There should always be a visible means of appeal in any appraisal system. This is often done through one or two 'grandparent' figures in the organization, i.e. senior or top managers, apart from those doing the appraisal, who can give a more objective view if necessary.

I have found such a system easy to design and apply at all levels of the organization – from managing director to the part-time workers. The use of the same behaviours, but different targets, from top to bottom of an organization also reinforces the organizational culture strongly. It may seem a heavy and complex system to install and maintain at first sight. My experience is that it is not. If the staff are asked to help in its design, their commitment to it ensures that it becomes easy to install and maintain – and well worth the investment if it changes the culture and behaviours to those of a learning organization.

I am keen on 'performance in job' as the basis of a robust appraisal system. Figure 2.3 outlines the basic process of appraisal. But it takes more than this to make an appraisal system part of the organization's process of learning and transforming itself. What is learned from individuals and groups needs to be fed into the broader overview of the organization's quality and volume of performance, structure and processes. A simple piece of computer software can monitor trends and not just identify developmental needs and cultural shifts in the organization, but also help ask questions regarding the appropriateness of such structural elements of the manage-

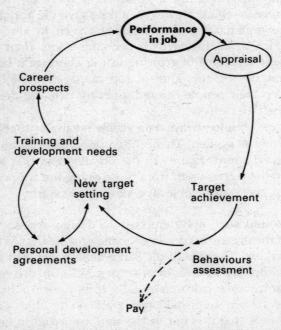

Figure 2.3 The basic appraisal process

ment of people as selection procedures, job descriptions, pay levels and reward packages, organizational structures and the effectiveness of organizational processes. This holistic system of appraisal is shown in Figure 2.4.

In Chapter 3 I shall return to the idea of using information from such sources as the appraisal system to reinforce the strategic objectives, operational targets and culture of an organization.

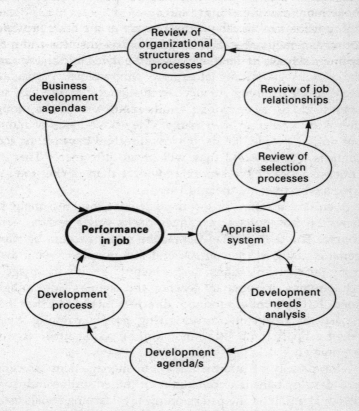

Figure 2.4   The holistic appraisal process

The Map of Current Resources for Development

THE SWING FROM TEACHING BACK TOWARDS LEARNING

Although the United Kingdom has the most diverse and developed provision for management education and development of any country, it is sadly not an integrated system and is, therefore, difficult for the uninitiated to map. This fragmentation means that most directors have little idea of the range and depth of the available provision. In this section I shall do my best to draw the map for you so that you may make more discriminating choices.

Top teams are usually vaguely aware of the State provision for management education in terms of the business and management schools in the university and polytechnic sectors, and the various governmental agency programmes, particularly those of the Training Agency. In this latter case the vast size often leads to the response 'I've heard of them even though they keep changing their name. They have loads of money but not for people like us.' Unless directors have strong local contacts in this world they will know little more. This is a criticism more of the service providers than of the potential clients who they are meant to serve.

A crude caricature of top management thinking about the range of development resources has a single answer – the course. The strong belief is that the main medium of managerial learning is 'the course', and that people are sent away from their organizations to 'be taught' – with its image of schoolrooms, a dominant teacher and exams. More enlightened, but still underinformed, directors might add that there is also an aspect of courses giving people working well a bit of a break (with its connotation of taking time off work legitimately).

This paucity of information about management education and development is undoubtedly of the education industry's own making. It has helped reinforce the 'learning equals teaching and courses' model over the decades. This stereotype is patently untrue. To educate oneself both the individual's skill in learning and good teachers are needed. The pendulum has been stuck on the teaching side for too long, particularly in secondary and tertiary education. However, it is beginning to change. Now that the clients are demanding more personal, real-time and flexibly delivered management education it finds itself stuck with its inflexible syllabuses, timetables, terms, mass teaching, lack of quality controls and dated delivery methods. This has been reinforced in the potential participants' minds through their acceptance of such an educational process since they were around 10 years old. It seems paradoxical that freer, experimental, ideas-based learning methods are deemed normal until 10 years old but then 'real teaching' takes over until one is well into one's late twenties. By then remedial action is needed to restimulate learning as a natural process in the individual – the majority of the alternatives to the State education provision are precisely geared to doing that.

True education is through the development of the whole person to make maximum use of his or her aptitudes and aspirations. The acquisition of knowledge is important, but not necessarily paramount. Skills and attitudes are of as much importance as knowledge in creating competence. In an information-based society it can be argued that the ability to ask the discriminating question and then have the skill of information retrieval is of more importance than being able to regurgitate the knowledge itself. Specialist learning, often acquired by rote, and its consequent thinking styles of convergence and overdeveloped judgement (these processes leading to analysis-paralysis), seem a perversion of the natural learning process. There is now a trend against overspecialization at all levels of society, allowing that basic numeracy and literacy – verbal, written and visual – are the building blocks from which everything is then learned. Hence the trend to such processes as 'project-based learning', 'action learning' and 'self-managed learning' for managers. In all of these the ability to link

55

personal development with real-time puzzle and problem-solving at the team and organizational levels is fundamental to its effectiveness.

THE MAPS
What maps can be drawn of the wider educational field so that well-informed decisions can be made and cost-effective ways followed to develop our people? I have concentrated mainly on the development of managers in this section but the process and much of the content is applicable to all sectors of an organization.

Keeping in mind the need for personal development agreements linked to personal time and money budgets between the individual and the organization, it is wise to start at the most cost-effective processes and then work towards the processes absorbing more time and money. It will be noted that teaching and courses are heavy on both time and money.

Self-Study – Newspapers, Journals and Books
This is often a totally forgotten means for helping people to develop. In its simplest form it can be as obvious as ensuring that relevant professional journal and newspaper articles are circulated and, most importantly, discussed on a regular basis. This also helps break the fear of being 'caught' reading or thinking at one's desk. It can be designed as a group learning process for which time, however short, is budgeted. (This has worked successfully in one case, outlined in Example 2.2.)

In its more advanced form regular reading and discussion of articles can be extended to books. There is a piece of corporate folklore that 'managers do not read'. This has been true to the extent that theirs is ultimately a verbal culture and the skills of reading can be eroded alarmingly unless regularly reinforced (as shown in Example 2.3). But the generation of people educated after the 1944 Butler Education Act are now reaching directoral positions in British organizations. Their education is wider than that of many of their predecessors,

---

Example 2.2 Making time to study and think

The new executive team of a major manufacturing company took over when it was in serious trouble. They had one year to turn it round or, they were told in a forceful way, it would be closed down. Their first instincts were to go into 'hands-on' mode to analyse and then try to rectify all the problems themselves. It took just two months for them to realize that this way led to ruin and that they had to delegate the puzzle-solving to their middle managers and supervisors. They were then free to face the strategic problems. But they had little idea of what to do. It was decided that really to be able to talk with each other they should take a half day per month off-site. To structure the process they agreed to cut out two or three newspaper or journal items each over the month, and be ready to talk about the likely effect on the business of each item. Whilst this felt strange at first it made legitimate the time spent reading and thinking about their strategic positioning. Three years later these 'awaydays' are a key part of the strategic development process of these directors and their company.

Example 2.3 Literacy and top managers

Whilst running a senior management development programme I was approached by an international group of participants who wanted to improve their reading skills through 'speed reading'. I had anticipated this to be a simple process. It was not. On testing them to get the base measure from which we could improve the skill I was surprised to find that their speed and comprehension was below the national average. They were surprised too. They were intelligent people and felt awkward that they had lost their earlier skills. It took some 12 hours of work to get them up to 800 words per minute and 90 per cent comprehension. But the deeper issue was why they had got into this position. We did some research and found that they were in a very verbal and action-orientated culture – what people said had higher priority than what was written. Over the years they lost their fluency in reading, but it had not mattered that much. However, it had led them into some dangerous behaviours. When reports came on to their desks, which happened all the time, they tended to look at the beginning and end for a synopsis. If it was there it was read. If not, then they tended to telephone each other and, unless one of them had read it, agreed what they thought was there. Their decisions were often taken on the basis of mutual ignorance.

---

and sadly to some of their successors. They do read, especially short, concise, informed and witty pieces – and they are skilled at debating and using writings for their specific needs. As management books continue to climb the publishers' bestseller lists worldwide perhaps we may even see the resurrection of the Victorian reading holiday in modern, corporate form.

Distance Learning and Open Learning

Britain is undoubtedly the world leader in this field. Distance learning has many forms but the essence is the transmission of study material through the mass media, whether post, television, radio or a mixture of these; work is undertaken on specific assignments; and these are assessed by a tutor situated at some distance from the learner.

The classic example is the Open University (OU), which Harold Wilson, who promoted the launching of the OU, said was the greatest achievement of his Government. The idea was to make university-level education available to those who had not had the opportunity to use it when they were in their late teens. These would include people from disadvantaged backgrounds, home-bound folk, people temporarily out of the labour market, and people who just wanted to better themselves. It is truly 'open', i.e. it does not have entry requirements. It uses the classic techniques of the correspondence course with the best of BBC TV and radio. Its material is carefully designed and tested, and scored by an experienced tutor.

The OU ensures that, unlike many other distance-learning facilities, each participant has a locally available tutor who can deal with both the technical content of the course and the learning processes of the individual. This adds a developmental edge to what otherwise might become a teaching dominated process. It awards degrees, both undergraduate and postgraduate. Its popularity is immense and its courses are very cheap. It has tapped the aspirations of people who would otherwise feel for ever trapped because they had 'missed out' on further education. As we move into an age where the state education system has failed to produce 'well-educated' people this national investment is likely to prove a wise one. Some companies recognize this and are using the Open University as a strategic training resource (Example 2.4 highlights this).

Example 2.4 The demand for open learning

When we produced the Open University's 'Effective Manager' programme we had expected a modest reaction from those managers who missed out in their management education. Whilst we were sure there were many tens of thousands of these we had expected them to be rather coy about coming forward. The advertisements went in the press and the first post brought thousands of replies. They mounted up from there to our delight and consternation. A raw nerve had been touched in British managers. The programme was so popular that other programmes were brought on stream rapidly. This has led to the founding of the Open Business School. Now major corporations pay for their executives to study through self-help via the Open Business School to re-educate themselves.

The OU model is being emulated across the world, particularly in Australia and China. In management education terms it has spawned similar activities from Henley Management College and such universities as Strathclyde, Aston, Warwick, etc. These offer Masters programmes and, in some cases, are helping companies with packages of continuous professional development within the company. The organization often pays the course cost and gives some of the time, provided that the staff member gives some of their free time as well.

In a modified form distance learning is being followed in the United Kingdom by the Open College, which transmits via television, videotapes and printed material, both technical training and specific skills development – from hands-on electronic engineering to the more strategic China Business Briefing.

Boss-Generated Development

This is a highly cost-effective personal development process yet it is often overlooked. It takes only a small amount of time, on a regular basis, to do the things I list below. With the decrease in labour availability in future, can you afford *not* to spend ten minutes a day doing the following?

COACHING, QUESTIONING AND FEEDBACK

Setting mutually agreed targets with individuals and teams, planning how to achieve them, then delegating the authority to get on with it and monitoring but not intervening in the reality – 'the eyes on and hands off' approach – is the mark of the learning leader. The essence of development through coaching, questioning and counselling is to ensure that a system of regular and rigorous feedback is set up and maintained so that each party can report what they saw occurring, deviations from plans analysed, volume and quality standards set, and the views of each expressed about any blockages that need to be cleared. This can be as simple as *The One Minute Manager*[17] notion of one minute's praise, one minute's criticism per person per day.

However complex the problem it needs to be remembered that this is coaching, not teaching. Like modern sports coaches the essence is not in telling people what and how to do something, but in getting them to develop, through regular questioning, a closer and closer focus on the way they generate feedback in themselves, and refine their targets and quality. This is another example of the use of discriminating questions in action.

I believe that this is the most powerful and cost-effective of all the development methods. Many directors state that they do not have time to get involved in such a process. This is disproved by those who have experimented and created time to coach their people. It was found to take remarkably little time, and once up and running the amount of regular input was almost homeopathic in dosage – very much the *One*

Minute Manager approach. The benefits were immense as people took more responsibility for their work volume and quality, and this ensured more time for the director to get on with the strategic leadership of the organization.

COUNSELLING

This well-known technique is in many ways a less specific form of coaching. Rather than focus on a fixed goal the process is for the other party, the member of staff, to explore their problems, the context in which these are set and possible solutions via a questioning process initiated by their boss or colleague.

Whilst it is a well-known method it is not widely and regularly used by directors, perhaps because it requires a more nurturing, empathetic approach – being able to put oneself in the other's position and start from where they are, rather than tell them what you think they should be doing. Action points come at the end of the counselling process and are generated by the counsellee, which can frustrate the more action-orientated bosses. This can, therefore, be seen as a soft process. It is not, and requires great skill to enable a person to explore their position well. I have noticed that it comes more easily from those people who have to command large numbers of people. Usually they have to learn it intuitively and are often startled when they find they have been counselling most of their working life.

MENTORING

Mentoring has been in vogue for many years, particularly in the United States. It has had a growing number of UK adherents in the last decade. The idea is a sound one – that a person usually more senior to you is given responsibility to bring you on in the company to make the best of your talents. This person is not the line manager of the mentee but someone in another department and often quite senior in the organization. They help the broader induction and inclusion into the organization and take a wider view of that inclusion than just the immediate job.

In a sense the mentor is the 'patron' of this individual and, used wisely, this can be of immense help in career development. Mentors are not always formally assigned and some people simply seek out a wise old owl they have met and respect inside the company or outside it – an old teacher or a family friend.

But there can be problems when mentoring is formally established in an organization. Patrons can become patronizing if they are not committed to the process, or have their own motivation for mentoring an individual. If mentees do not then fit in with their plans they can be in trouble and will need to rely on their line manager and the appraisal system to see them through. However, the line manager may not wish to confront a senior manager in another department. Your mentor will be subject to the usual political rise and fall of any organization, and if you are seen to be closely associated with him or her you will unwittingly have to ride that switchback too (Example 2.5).

JOB ROTATION

This is another frequently overlooked boss-generated developmental process. Some organizations have specific job performance indicators, particularly for their fast-track people, which are designed around job rotation. For example, they will specify that someone likely to make director level will have had significant profit centre responsibility by, say, the age of 28 and will have run an overseas subsidiary by the age of 35, etc. The indicators for a specific organization will be unique. All I will say here is that they need to be a key part of the basis of the manpower planning system of the organization. The benefits of job rotation have been that they help broaden people and give them new challenges as part of their developmental process. Whereas this has so far been mainly for the fast-track managers, it is now being reviewed as a key aspect of keeping

---

Example 2.5 The problem with mentoring

A bright young personnel executive had been most impressed with the first boss he had. They worked together well in their company and when the boss moved on it was only a short time before the young executive was delighted to be asked to follow. They did well in their next company and created a name for themselves in the industry. The boss was headhunted a couple of years later. True to form the executive followed a few months later. Things went well for three years until they were taken over by another company. This company had a rough, tough and brutal culture and did not take well to the nurturing approach of the boss and executive. Within months the boss was made redundant. The executive stayed on and was seen to do very well, but was always referred to in conversation as being the old boss's protégé. When a new round of cuts was proposed the executive went, despite everyone agreeing that he was doing a good job, and that the person who would take over was known not to be suitable. When questioned as to why this decision was taken the new director admitted that it was simply to 'get rid of all signs of the old boss'.

---

scarce people in the organization at all levels and, as such, fits neatly into the *self-development agreement* idea. The Japanese have long understood this and have developed job rotation as an organizational way of life to encourage inclusion and consensus throughout their organizations. It is also seen as a way of combating complacency and ensuring that most people are multi-skilled. Specialists in Japanese organizations tend to be few and far between, and very specialist indeed.

Courses

OPEN COURSES
This is the stereotype of how all management development takes place. However, I hope that I have shown that they are not the major vehicles for holistic learning. They help with the acquisition of knowledge rather than the deployment of it in a competent manner. As such they have important but limited utility. The boom in the running of management

courses in the last decade has shown the apparently insatiable demand for them. Whether they are used wisely and cost-effectively is open to doubt. I have tried to outline below my approach to them.

Work I did with a management college in the early 1980s showed that on a series of specialist open (to all comers) courses the rank order of priorities of those attending was given as:

(i)   Getting the views and experiences of managers outside my company.
(ii) Getting the views of managers outside my industry.
(iii) Gaining new knowledge, techniques and skills.
(iv) Making contacts for future career possibilities.
(v)   Having a break from my usual routine.

I think that this is a realistic assessment of the utility of open courses. They are useful for generating different perspectives, different views, encouraging debate and a broader under-standing, as well as for transmitting technical information and skills development. They can cause potential problems for non-learning organizations because they expose their people to a range of opportunities which they may not have con-sidered, so the chances either of having discontented people return, or of losing them, are raised. Sadly, it is only in a few cases that they are used by an organization to give an indi-vidual or team time to think and debate.

Participants are still mainly 'sent' on a course rather than using it as a conscious part of their developmental process. When asked at the start of a course 'Why are you here?' it is still common to hear such responses as 'It was my turn', 'No one else was available and we did not want to lose the cancellation fee', or the backhanded compliment of 'It sounded interesting and I needed a bit of a break.'

The market for open courses has been dropping in the last decade as the total number of courses rises. The ability to cross-communicate with different colleagues has been reduced across companies and industries. This seems to be because of the rise of the other main type of course. Whether this will be rebalanced in the long term as demand swings back has yet to be seen.

TAILORED OR IN-COMPANY COURSES
These are usually little more than the open course with the audience drawn from a single department, company or group. Minor 'tailoring' is made to add cases or speakers about the appropriate industry or company. At their best they can be highly effective at focusing the minds of key individuals, and teams, on specific topics and can energize people to action when back in the organization. At their worst they can be ways of reinforcing existing company prejudices and blocking contradictory information and changes in the processes and contexts of other companies and industries. Tailored courses are the big growth element of management development at present. Let us hope they will fall back to their rightful place as one method in a portfolio of developmental processes to be used by discriminating learning leaders.

OUTDOOR TRAINING COURSES
The other growth phenomenon of the last decade in the United Kingdom has been the rapid growth of outdoor training courses. These range from survival training in the wilds of Scotland in midwinter with SAS-schooled trainers, via adventure training courses which feature action-based problem-solving whilst moving across country, through wargames with paint-filled 'splat guns', to sports coaching adapted for management at such national centres as Bisham Abbey.

I must declare a prejudice here. I think that all of these are good ways of getting out of the usual routines and challenging oneself in ways one would normally not dream of. However, as they tend to concentrate on the action and not so much on feedback and learning they seem of limited utility. Sales teams will for ever wish to play wargames, cover their opponents with paint and swing on ropes over rushing rivers. But should middle-aged managers risk coronaries trying to abseil off cliffs? One occasion sticks in my mind. There were twenty senior directors of an international engineering company crossing a large lake in the Midlands. Training had been given on how to get out of a kayak if it turned over. When they were all in the middle of the lake a freak squall sprang up and the whole lot turned over. What had not been appreciated was how much longer it took directors with paunches actually to abandon their canoes. Luckily it was possible to rescue them all but the consequences of losing some of their key people was brought home strongly to the company.

A growing criticism of the outdoor courses is that they are leading to more erosion of the physical environment. Most, but not all, of these courses take place on private land. This is no guarantee against erosion but they should at least not affect the public domain. However, queries are being raised as to how much this type of course can be promoted before permanent damage is done to some of our wilder heritage.

One final point on courses. There has been an upward spiral of the daily prices of courses often ahead of inflation. Course running has become a highly profitable part of the education industry and rates of between £100 and £600 per person per day are quoted regularly. This can make a hole in any training and development budget. So the use of courses, particularly residential ones, needs careful consideration in the light of what might be possible through self-study and boss-generated development.

Action Learning – The Integration of Developmental Activities
Action learning[12] is one of the British overseas successes which is hardly known in the United Kingdom. It uses the live real-time problems of an organization to form the vehicle by which people develop themselves and their organization simultaneously. Its effects in Belgium, Egypt, Australia, Ghana, India, etc, are well known in these countries. Indeed action

learning is acknowledged by the Japanese Productivity Council[18] as being a major source of inspiration for *quality circles* through Reg Revans's work on learning circles in the British National Coal Board after nationalization in 1947.

Revans has suffered the fate of a prophet in his own land. But the action learning idea has taken root in the United Kingdom again and organizations as diverse as the General Electric Company, Foster Wheeler, the North West Water Board and Bradford Metropolitan Council are using it to create simultaneous development processes.

The essence is as simple, and complex, as human learning itself. The focus is for human beings to learn from understanding the way they face a real-time problem, collect information rather than data, reflect on it, plan how to solve it, experiment with possible ways of creating change, and then, most importantly, take responsibility for delivering that change. To do this they need both regular and rigorous, constructively critical support. This comes from others attempting similar changes in their organization – the 'comrades in adversity'. The argument is that the information and energy needed to create organizational change and solve present problems is already within that organization. The challenge is to release it and move it to where it can be used. Learning how to take responsibility to do that is reinforced by the help of others in the same position – the action learning group or 'set'.

This simple and elegant notion integrates personal, team and organizational development because it focuses on crucial organizational issues. By using intelligently naïve people with responsibility for creating change through action, this approach develops them on all fronts in a way that no other method can. It does not exclude the opportunistic use of any other developmental method provided it helps to resolve the organizational problems. I shall say more about this sort of approach in Chapter 3.

Innovations in Development
Before we leave this chapter I shall outline two other aspects which are beginning to emerge as additions to the developmental portfolio. One is very high-tech, the other more an idea whose time has yet to come.

INTERACTIVE AND EXPERT SYSTEMS
Information technology has developed to a point where it is possible to take the best knowledge, attitudes and skills from your experts and codify these into an electronic database. This can be used in two ways. It can form the base of a continuing debating and updating process for the experts themselves. This ensures that they are state-of-the-art. It has also revealed some errors or lacunae in the thinking processes and behaviours of the experts which can be rectified relatively easily. On the other hand the database can feed the best thoughts and actions of the experts directly into the training system of the organization so that it is as up to date as possible. The material is presented in both visual (moving and still pictures) and numerical form.

This is usually achieved through an interactive videodisc. The data is pressed on to the laser disc and then interacts with the user. It is not a linear vehicle like a videotape where the teaching has to be predetermined. Rather, it can respond to any question asked of it. So the key is to ask discriminating questions of the data, i.e. to learn how to turn data into information. The advanced forms of interactive discs have the ability to monitor the learning and thinking styles of the user and both to assess and to prompt feedback about the appropriateness of the user's approach. Some discs have different styles of learning built into the software so that the user can experiment and learn how to use a more appropriate style. These are early days for interactive expert systems and at present the initial costs are relatively high, but the reduction in old-style trainer costs and improvements in the retention of the information learned show hopeful signs for the future.

CONTINUOUS PROFESSIONAL DEVELOPMENT

Continuous professional development has been used by the professions for some decades. It is a key notion in that it assumes that no one can stand still and rest on their previous learning, no matter how comprehensive and deep it was. Therefore, one needs to design a system of assessment and development where it is natural to seek always to improve, rather than to 'plateau'. For directors this is becoming an important issue as professional liability under the Company Act of 1986 redraws the responsibilities of directors and ensures that they are professionally liable for the actions of their organizations.

Developing Our Organizations

Why Do We Need To Do It?

The Intellectual Argument – Change, Chaos and Learning
We develop organizations for two simple reasons. First, because without development they die. Second, there are financial and spiritual rewards for so doing. You cannot get more basic than that.

It is a fundamental law of ecology that for any organism to survive, its rate of learning must be equal to, or greater than, the rate of change in its environment.[12] This is expressed as:

$$L \geqslant C$$

and the formula holds good from the meanest single cell to the most complex transnational organization. Stated in this way I have yet to meet a director, or manager, who would disagree with the idea. Indeed they are typically all for it as they see this formula as the building block of organizational development theory. Curiously, it is not taught as being central to the current body of knowledge in any of the business or management schools. At this level of abstraction it also makes great sense to them that they become learning leaders of their developing organization.

Being action orientated they want to know 'how can I do this – now?' There are many ways of starting but I remind them that development is a process of nurturing and bringing out, rather than one of rushing on and hammering in. I even tease them a bit that 'development' derives from the Latin 'volupe', so are they ready to handle the voluptuousness, or sensory pleasure, associated with developing their organizations?

CHANGE

Change has become recognized as a necessary component of modern management thought and action. It has even become modish in the management education industry. It is in danger in some quarters of becoming an end in itself. This is most unwise. Chairman Mao's theory of 'continuous revolution' may be a modern necessity as the external environment of the organization changes so rapidly in terms of its political, economic, social, physical and technological dynamics, but there is then no need to increase the rate of turbulence by overemphasizing the change side of the $L \geqslant C$ formula. Change is a natural, evolutionary condition and needs to be balanced in learning leaders' heads by the other side of the formula – *learning*. I will deal with this in greater detail in Chapter 4.

CHAOS

Let me deal here with some aspects of change and turbulence, about which a great deal has been written but not that much researched as to the basis of such ideas. In the scientific world there is great excitement because over the past 15 years a new branch of science – chaos – has emerged.[19] With the apparently increasing precision with which particle scientists, microbiologists, mathematicians and chemists were working it looked as though they would be able to measure and explain totally our physical world. Even the great imponderables of quantum mechanics and relativity, the creation of the universe and other such cosmic dimensions seemed to be within touch of explanation through the application of well-honed scientific methods. Admittedly, there were the occasional freak readings in most experiments but these were seen as statistically insignificant, so they did not need to concern the researchers.

There are scientists, typically and significantly those who have more than one discipline, who pointed out that despite the huge increase in the precision of measurement in some areas, they still could not explain very simple, everyday phenomena. As scientists felt increasingly at a dead end looking either cross-eyed at the micro-world or starry-eyed at the macro-world, the criticism from outsiders of their inability to explain everyday phenomena hit home, and prompted some individuals to determine to seek explanations. We cannot, for example, forecast weather accurately, nor predict the precise patterns of convection in a cup of tea, nor can we predict the behaviour of commodity markets, nor the behaviour of a child's swing.

Scientists studying apparently stable systems found that, through infinitesimally small shifts in the behaviour of the systems, they can fall into apparent chaos. Paradoxically, they found that within this chaos there seemed to be strange and elegant patterns which repeated themselves at all levels of focus, and seemed to have elements of predictability within them. These are now being studied through research efforts all over the world and seem to offer more hope for helping directors deal with an uncertain environment than, say, *Catastrophe Theory*,[20] which offered so much and seems to have delivered so little. The good news is that a combination of chaoticists and our increasing ability through electronics to search for visual patterns via our new databases should allow us to have some useful working rules within the next decade.

The bad news is that directors and managers are not yet developed for such approaches. They have had enough difficulty coming to terms with the notion of continuous change in a turbulent environment without wishing to grapple with the ideologically unacceptable notion of chaos. This is due in great part to our secondary and tertiary education being through specialization, rather than integration and systems thinking. Revans's plea for wise leaders who can ask good questions of clever people is echoed by one of the great writers on scientific development, Thomas Kuhn.[21]

> Under normal conditions the research scientist is not an innovator but a solver of puzzles, and the puzzles on which he concentrates are just those which he believes can be both stated and solved within the existing scientific tradition.

I think that the same applies to management and leadership, and helps explain our willingness to return to our old specialist jobs when faced with adversity, uncertainty and chaos.

Becoming a learning leader is about developing the creativity, skill and courage to get into our strategic corporate psychological helicopter, transcend the current perception of the problem and then throw new light and perspective on the problem; to redefine the problem so that it becomes soluble, or at least can be moved on – i.e. to change the mindset, the paradigms, of those responsible for solving it.

LEARNING

What has this to do with organizational learning? Lots. Returning to the $L \geqslant C$ formula, it fascinates me that 'learning' is the variable counterposed to 'change'. This was never taught me at my management school. I spent years working on finance, marketing, personnel and production, and followed all sorts of functional byways and dead ends. Is there something wrong with the $L \geqslant C$ formula? Is it both necessary and sufficient? If so, then is there something wrong with our present view of management and leadership? I have argued the case for some 20 years and have recently begun to find some slightly unnerving allies. Until now my mindset had been to see such folk as corporate lawyers and financiers – hard-eyed people with few constructive emotions and 'no bowels', to quote James Thurber – as the virtual class enemies of developers. Suddenly things are changing as the notion of $L \geqslant C$ is being seen as a necessary component for corporate health and survival. At its crudest, they are increasingly aware that there is good money in the learning of an organization. There always has been, but few realized it. Suddenly subjects previously seen through prevailing mindsets as soft and wimpish, such as intellectual property and codification of learning, are now appearing on the corporate agenda.

●● Intellectual property and its rights

When I talk with boards or top teams, or at a public conference, there is now a noticeable enthusiasm to learn more about *intellectual property rights* and apply the ideas which I am propounding. What is going on? It is certainly not a breakthrough on the chaos side – yet. The change in attitude shows hard-edged reconsiderations about the *value* of learning; there is now a clearer view that survival, growth and money are in it.

Until now the ability to spot the learning occurring in our organizations – through the employment and actions of people in whom we have invested time and money – has been negligible. Different functions, departments and teams have tended to find their own solutions to their problems and puzzles. They have codified – committed to a system of recording – the learning in as precise or lax a manner as they thought necessary and then this coding was usually consigned to the filing cabinet, disk or portfolio. This lack of systems thinking is similar to the problem of the appraisal non-systems thinking which I have already outlined in Chapter 2. There are diverse inputs, little rigour in coding, and no output that transcends the immediate functional boundaries. There is, therefore, nothing which allows the organization to adapt its processes or rate of learning.

Why bother with what at first sight seems a rather mechanical and boring process which only tidies up after the action-related 'real' work of manufacture or service delivery? Why worry about all the bits of learning that occurred on the way, or could have been derived from debriefings afterwards? The answer is found now in the international courts. IBM is battling with competitors over the right to use its operating systems. Apple Computers is locked in a similar fight with its competitors. Toblerone, the Swiss chocolate company, has invested large sums in producing high-quality chocolate bars, marketing them and selling them worldwide to create an upmarket image. It is now fighting others in the courts to ensure that its triangular design remains unique. Levi jeans are fighting court cases against other manufacturers to try and ensure that they cannot use copper rivets in their jeans. These latter cases may sound trivial but the economic consequences for such global brands and products can reach hundreds of millions of dollars, and for high-tech manufacturers in the billions.

The battles are about protecting the investment made in the learning of their organizations. Specifically, they concern their *intellectual property* and the *rights* that can be established, nationally and internationally, over it. Once established, then any competitor will have to pay for the right to do things their way. This is heady stuff. Whoever thought that leading and managing an organization was an intellectual process of life and death? The vast majority of directors would rather be dead than 'intellectual'. They may well have their wish as the old-style 'macho managers' get their come-uppance in the 'new order' world of chaos, intellect, change and learning.

What are these intellectual property rights (IPRs)? There are five legal categories acknowledged in most of the world's legal systems:

- Patents
- Registered designs
- Copyright
- Trademark
- Servicemark

to which can be added in certain categories in some countries:

- Trade secrets

At the international level the meaning of these terms is fought out at the General Agreement on Tariffs and Trade (GATT), or the United Nations' affiliate World Intellectual Property Organization – they are talking about big money. Pilkington, the British glassmaker who invented float glass, calculates that it made far more money by licensing its process around the world to its 35 competitors than it would have done by building its own plants to service a world market. In the United States the Batelle Institute, essentially an ideas research and development institute, grew from 30 employees and a revenue of $3.5 million in 1925 to 8,000 employees and a turnover of $610 million in 1987. In the United Kingdom Thorn–EMI has traditionally kept its intellectual property – rights to songs such as 'Happy Birthday to You', 'Singing in the Rain' and 'The Warsaw Concerto', and to films – off its balance sheet. Now there is pressure, as with brands, to put them on to the balance sheet. This should make the company a less easy takeover target. As the analysts reckon that this will add between £1 billion and £4 billion, it can easily be seen what a difference valuing intellectual property can make. One major electronics company is now going back through the design ideas of its scientists and technicians rejected over the last two decades looking for ideas in which it has already invested but has not established its intellectual property rights.

It is noticeable even in countries famous for their (often illegal) copying of others' products that people are realizing that future wealth lies in the creation of intellectual property as well as the exploitation of it. That is where the real added-value and cash-streams are. It is a sign of economic maturity when a country invests in this creation process rather than copying. So, for example, Hong Kong is now building more universities, polytechnics and science parks, and will reinforce the output of these by introducing much tougher intellectual property laws, despite the old Confucian notion that 'there should be no tax on knowledge'. It is already much more difficult to get fake Rolex watches, Gucci luggage or Lacoste shirts on the streets there. Soon it should be virtually impossible.

●● Learning leaders and intellectual property

Central to the intellectual property issue is the ability to capture, codify and diffuse in a useful and profitable form the learning of the organization. This is where the need to develop the role of learning leaders is paramount for the organization to have the chance to survive and grow. Learning occurs all over organizations. The problem is that there are so few systems for valuing it and capturing it.

What can be done? Some organizations have turned over whole floors to create new departments of intellectual property. In these designers, engineers, line managers and lawyers review the legal position of current products and services. They are finding often that surprisingly few are covered by IPRs, thereby leaving them open for competitors to copy, or even register the design or process, in as many countries as possible. In the worse case there is the possibility that you would have to buy back the rights to intellectual property that you have created but not protected.

At present the messiness and imprecision of intellectual property law makes it a lawyer's paradise and this puts off many directors. However, it is increasingly necessary to register your organization's learning. You have, after all, invested in it and in your people – the only resource you have that is capable of learning. It is sheer misunderstanding and lack of leadership that has allowed the present laxity and lack of systems to develop. If one's rate of learning is to be equal to, or greater than, the rate of environmental change, now is the time to respond to this rapidly changing part of the environment.

●● Brands

A noticeable spin-off from the new interest in intellectual property is the focus on brands. It has long been understood that, especially for commodity suppliers like the oil companies, food producers, cigarette makers, etc, it is both possible and necessary to build customer loyalty to a specific brand. This has two advantages. First, it gives some stability in an otherwise fickle marketplace through having loyal customers who can perceive tangible differences between one brand and another. This allows for more reliable planning and product development for the marketeers, and it often allows a premium price to be charged or, at worst, no discount to be granted.

Second, as brands and customer loyalty are built over the years they are seen to have a positive and quantifiable value to the organization. This is logical as they are one manifestation of the investment in the learning of that organization. Many organizations who have pursued such a route have tended to concentrate on brands, products and market share as manifestations of the annual operating results of the business. They are shown on the profit and loss account in the annual report. Now another trend is emerging as the accountants and lawyers argue that these are long-term investments in markets and learning and should, therefore, be accounted as part of the balance sheet because they are a strategic investment.

The brand is a specific asset of the organization, they argue. This is a matter of debate amongst top managers at present. Rank Hovis McDougall (RHM) revalued its balance sheets at a stroke in 1988 from £250 million to some £928 million through taking such brands as 'Hovis', 'Mr Kipling' and 'Bisto' on to the balance sheet. It seems that for RHM the brands are worth more than the buildings and raw materials which produce them.

What is of particular interest to me is that this brings the valuing of an organization's learning into a highly tangible form. It is noticeable that the practice is moving from commodity products to 'designer' products. This is easily seen in such areas as clothes, jewellery, perfumes, etc. But it is also appearing in such apparently commodity products as bottled water where, for example, David Hockney graces the Abbey Well label, making it truly a 'designer water'.

●● Branding and the service industries

Branding and servicemarks show that the practice is stretching into the service industries, which, some argue, rely entirely on the ability of their customer-facing staff to add value through continuous learning and development. This has been understood by retailers and airlines and is now being acknowledged in such apparently unresponsive fields as financial and professional services. As the rate of external change increases rapidly – deregulation and international competition being encouraged by Governments and the EC – they are having continuously to transform their organizations to deliver higher quality and more relevant services. Not all of them will make it. Those who do will have realized that the people with the ability to learn what their customers want, and who can respond rapidly to deliver it, will be those who continue to add value and profitability to the services of the organization and, ultimately, through the customers' increased perception of the quality of the services, their market share.

*The Practical Argument – The Changing Socio-Political
Environment of Organizations and its Effects on Learning Leaders*
The changes created by the Government through such political initiatives as privatization, deregulation, competitiveness, and price freedom, leading to the increased productivity of our organizations (public and private), have led to a massive change in British society. They are having knock-on effects in such countries as the United States, France, Italy, New Zealand, Australia, even China and the USSR. Whilst the cleaning of public and private Augean stables was necessary, the social consequences of these changes are less predictable for the long term. The implied management style has been 'macho' rather than a blend of achieving and nurturing. Consequently, the followership style has tended to be concerned with passivity or the negative aspects of recognition, and this reduces the nuturing climate. In turn this will cause problems as without nurturing – even a thin film will do – development cannot

take place. Such nurturing includes accepting that learners have to make mistakes in order to learn, and that they need rigorous feedback to reinforce what is learned. Without this there is little systematic learning. In this case one is then left wondering what has been achieved in the hearts and minds of the people not captured by their own self-interest. I shall return to this point when we are talking of creating the climate and culture of the learning organization in Chapter 4.

That the political and organizational environment has changed can be demonstrated easily. In 1976 I worked as a consultant with the Government's Training Services Agency to create a public discussion paper on the future of management development in the United Kingdom. As part of our work we surveyed a number of employers as to their aims in using management development. The results were surprisingly similar, regardless of industry or size of business.

At a more informal enquiry I repeated the questions amongst my clients over the period 1987–9, and then compared these results against the participants on my programmes carried out at the same time at the Institute of Directors. Again, the patterning was remarkably similar but the results were quite different. When comparing the two sets of results a distinct national culture change was noticeable (Table 3.1).

One can debate the 1988 results and whether they are a permanent mindset change or simply the results of the rigours of economic necessity, which will turn again as national wealth improves. My concern is that a focus, rather like the Government's, on short-term results (the feeling of needing to increase efficiency before organizational effectiveness) can end in the death of the organization. This can be achieved whilst apparently keeping up *earnings per share* (a current icon of top managers). Both sides will argue that without it you are dead. My position is that in an area where perceived quality of product or service, especially service, is paramount, then it is organizational effectiveness (a healthy relationship with the external environment) which ensures long-term survival and

Table 3.1 Reasons given by senior managers for pursuing management development in their organizations

	Rank order	
	1988	*1977*
To increase the efficiency of my organization	1	3
To increase the effectiveness of my organization	2	5
To encourage managers to take responsibility for their own development	3	6
To ensure a flow of competent managers	4	1
To give managers confidence in the exercise of their own function	5	2
To develop a common ethos	6	4

market share – the hard edge of the $L \geqslant C$ idea. It is quite possible for an organization to be simultaneously externally effective and internally inefficient. Many 'successful' organizations are and remain profitable and expanding by charging premium prices for their perceived quality. I know of none who is internally efficient and externally ineffective for more than a few years. The ideal is to be both internally efficient and externally effective – but none of us knows enough about the energizing and control of our 'chaotic' organizations to be able to do this easily.

If you compare the 1988 figures with those of 1977 in Table 3.1 then the rank order has virtually reversed. In 1988 the focus is on the effectiveness and efficiency of organizations; on the acknowledgement that individuals, not organizations, are responsible for their own development; on the idea that a flow of competent managers should exist but in truth is unlikely given the demographic situation; and the idea that there is a need to develop a common ethos (i.e. to ensure that only 'people like us' are allowed into our organizations) is only ranked at the end.

This gives some insight into the political times 14 years ago.

81

Then the main focus was on the need for managers to have confidence in exercising their own function. This is explained by remembering that this was the period when the trade unions were seen as having a major say in the Labour Government, and were demanding more and more labour legislation to rebalance the perceived historical imbalance of managerial control. They were challenging the 'right of managers to manage' and this led in 1979 to the 'Winter of Discontent' and the first Thatcher administration. The managers of 1977 were shell-shocked, disorientated and seemed doubtful of the continuation of the very role of managing if things went on the way they were. Their demoralization had been made worse by the wage freezes, the tax rises and the reduction in differentials, which meant that some of them were earning less than their staff.

The 'developing a common ethos' aspect is also a museum piece. This seemed to be the last fling of the notion that managers were essentially related to social (middle) class and so, effectively, were their industries. People inducted into management then had to be of a similar educational, social and often political background. Many of the courses run for such new managers, or potential managers, were of an undemanding intellectual or skills development content but were important checks as to whether 'our kind of people' had been selected so that they would not let the side down. The 'side' was not necessarily the organization but often a broader and amorphous group of 'people like us'. Rabid Marxists, people with handbags, those that ate their peas with a knife and those who could not hold their drink were usually out regardless of their performance in their job.

Things have certainly changed as selection procedures have become more geared to performance – 'doing' the managing role was assessed and rewarded rather than just 'being' a manager. When this was backed by decent information bases (via psychometric tests, etc) as well as the judgement of peers, then the situation became healthier. I have mentioned before the need for sufficient variety in top teams to allow for individual, team and organizational development. This need for differences throws into sharp profile the need to create a unifying 'common vision' of what we will strive for the future to be.

The most important reason for development in 1977 was the need to ensure the flow of competent managers. There was a mindset around of each organization needing to create its own pool of managerial talent, and skilled technical and administrative talent too, on which one could draw as and when needed. At a time of growing unemployment, and of managers who believed that 'the organization will look after our careers if we keep our noses clean', this was a workable model. It is not workable in the 1990s. The lack of good managerial talent (often hastened by the efficient but not effective, and therefore unwise, enforced early retirement of experienced managers) means that there are few 'pools' available. So everyone tries to poach from each other.

This notion of the need for a pool of talent in larger organizations was one of the early arguments of the Management Charter Initiative in 1987. It seemed at first hearing to be an attempt by the large UK-based companies to lock in talent through offering a type of contracted career path for their people, especially their graduates. However, the industrialists supporting the MCI did not seem to appreciate that other forces had been sharpening the awareness of managers that their organizations could never deliver a guaranteed career without direction of labour. This is socially unacceptable. So the responsibility for creating their careers has now been increasingly accepted as being that of individuals. Today only a very few organizations (some oil companies, a couple of international banks, a telecommunications company) have their 'heaven born' (their fast-track managers) on contracts which say, typically, that they must move anywhere in the world within 48 hours. In return for this they are given large rewards, often retirement between 50 and 55 years old, and a guarantee that their family will always be cared for by the company.

Such absolutism in contracts and careers is rare. The pendulum has swung the other way and we are seeing much more a mentality of project, or service, contracts (for specified periods with the organization) with the managers themselves accepting responsibility for their own development. Hence the enthusiasm for personal development agreements and the creation of information sources such as 'The Good Development Guide' which make best practice available easily to line managers.[22]

It is to the ideas behind the individual taking responsibility for his or her own development and the service contract that I wish now to turn. These pose a massive shift in the way we think about organizations because the ideas assume them to be more fragmented and more people-orientated than we have previously accepted. A reframing of what organizations are, and how they might operate, is under way internationally.

The Process of Organizational Development

It is not my intention here to go into detail about how organizations have been developed in the past. The processes of team-building, inter-teambuilding, changing organizational structures, processes, culture, styles and values are well recorded. 'New order' approaches to organizational development – integrated holistic approaches via action learning to create learning organizations – are suggested for the twenty-first century. I shall deal with these in Chapter 4. I will look at the nature of these 'new order' organizations first. (Example 3.1 contrasts the role of management in 'new order' organizations with those of the 'old order'.)

Example 3.1 From old order to new order organizations
The changing role of management in organizations can be described as:

Old order	New order
Production-based	Customer service-based
Structure-based	Process-based
Efficiency-orientated	Effectiveness-orientated
Conformist	Creative & responsive
Bureaucratic structure	Flexible structure
Job-orientated	People-orientated
Data-orientated	Information-orientated

'New Order' Organizations

INFORMATION-BASED ORGANIZATIONS

The typical large business 20 years hence will have fewer than half the levels of management of its counterpart today, and no more than a third of its managers. In its structure, and in its management problems and concerns, it will bear little resemblance to the typical manufacturing company circa 1950, which our textbooks still consider the norm. Instead it is far more likely to resemble organizations that neither the practising manager nor the management scholar pays much attention to today; the hospital, the university, the symphony orchestra. For like them, the typical business will be knowledge-based, an organization composed largely of specialists who direct and discipline their own performance through organised feedback from colleagues, customers and headquarters. For this reason, it will be what I call an 'information-based' organisation.[23]

This clear view of twenty-first-century organizations comes not from some bright, young, inexperienced thing determined to make their mark on the corporate futurology scene but from that octogenarian writer and professor Peter Drucker. This paragraph elegantly synthesizes many of the issues about which I have written so far. It helps us to focus on what our organizations might be like in the future. It also raises deeper questions as to whether we will have that many managers at all, or whether the process of management will become an integral part of all jobs in the organization.

The vital parts of Drucker's vision all have present-day roots. They are: more information systems to drive the knowledge-based organization; flatter organization structures (possibly of just four hierarchical levels – customer-facing staff, supervisors, managers and directors); multiple feedback loops for personal, team and organizational appraisal; and great emphasis on individual and personal communication and recognition, not just inside the organization but outside – by the customer and the social environment – as shown by the importance of Handy's 'byline' notion.

The organizational model is more of an interactive dynamic system than a well-oiled machine. This creates a problem in itself. For the majority of people, not just managers, their perception of the organization seems to be a cross between the inefficiencies and unquestioning behaviours of Charlie Chaplin's *Modern Times* and the chilling psychic prisons of Kafka's *The Trial* and *The Castle*. Both reinforce views of organizations as anti-individual, controlling to an unacceptable level and highly oppressive. There is no doubt that some organizations are consciously all of these. Most seem to have got there through lack of leadership, vision and creativity over a sustained period. They have drifted into this unhealthy organizational climate and cannot learn how to find a way out.

This feeling of organizations as black holes for humans – absorbing all known energy, hope and light – is common. To an extent it is paradoxical as, at the same time, it is these very organizations which have created so much of twentieth-century human progress. The specialization of work has allowed large numbers of people to undertake complex projects and create a synergistic output from their organizations. It can be argued that one of the great human triumphs of the twentieth century is the creation and mastery of modern bureaucracy. That may sound strange as 'bureaucracy' tends to be mouthed as a pejorative today. This is sad as the idea of the division of labour, and the rules and sanctions as described by Max Weber, allow us to do great things provided these organizations are led by humane thinkers and visionary learning leaders who can transcend the specialisms and view the organization and its objectives holistically. In unthinking and unlearning hands bureaucracies cause great harm. The challenge to learning leaders is to use the positive aspects of the notion of bureaucracy to achieve human ends rather than, as is so often found, to use humans for bureaucratic ends.

THE EDUCATED ORGANIZATION

Charles Handy's new book *The Age of Unreason*[24] pursues a similar theme to that of Peter Drucker. Rather than focus on 'information-based' organizations he looks at the likely values, culture and behaviours of people in the *new order* organizations and of the organizational forms evolving to meet this challenge. Like Drucker, Handy sees organizations as being composed increasingly of specialists or professionals – 'the educated organization'. He speculates on the future needs of such people and the processes of developing and retaining them. He thinks they gain most from the nature and quality of their work, rather than the mere fact of belonging to a specific organization. They therefore expect 'bylines', i.e. that their work will be recognized through public acknowledgement, whether this is having their name on the engine block of a car, being on the seemingly endless credits at the end of a TV programme, or being celebrated in the company magazine as the best team in the firm's total quality management programme.

This is the start of more subtle staff reward processes about which learning leaders need to take note. They certainly need to ensure that time and money budgets are derived through the appraisal system to allow both individual development and recognition of the results. But more than that they need to reframe the role, rights and duties of directors to ensure that the conditions exist in which people will do a quality job as second nature. Subsequently customers will perceive that quality and ultimately society may accept the organization as a responsible corporate citizen and a good employer. By so doing the organization completes the cycle and refines its ability to select and retain its people.

Handy suggests that the future organizational shape will not be the classical pyramid with its neat, hierarchical levels, but a clover leaf at the centre of which lies the 'core team' and from which radiate ever-changing workgroups and project teams. These are crucial to the organization at any point in time but may not be a continuing part of the business over the long term. They may, like many professionals, prefer service contracts for a specific project or job to a specific quality, over a specific time. They might have short-term contracts; be part-time workers; be physically present with the core team yet be self-employed; be working at a distance on projects; or be telecommuting via the new data networks. Some may act in a specialist adviser or consultant capacity to the organization on a fees basis. They may be seen rarely in the organization but, like all the other types of networkers, they are part of the organization. They have such an important part to play in reducing the overhead spend of organizations and in increasing its flexibility to respond rapidly to environmental change. They are becoming an increasingly important aspect of the design of twenty-first-century organizations.

This is a very different view from the twentieth-century idea of organizations as mechanical structures with little adaptability once they are designed. In the twentieth century people have had to fit the organizations as best they could. The opposite will be true in the next century. This offers great opportunities and will create big cultural and behavioural problems for directors. The change in mindset of what our organizations are, and how they might be organized and managed, is the driving force for the development of learning leaders. It is to grapple with such issues that they need the time to think and act strategically. It will be a period of increased risks, but as the Chinese character for risk can also be translated as 'dangerous opportunity' this latter outlook seems a good mindset for the learning leaders of the twenty-first century.

Developing the Change Process in the Organization

If change is now the one constant for organizations, how can we encourage them to face up to this? It seems such a daunting prospect to most directors, although a liberating one if it can be achieved. One thing that has been learned painfully about organizational change is that it cannot be attempted all at once. It is both an evolutionary and a truly revolutionary process – each revolution bringing it back to the same place but, hopefully, one notch higher on the developmental spiral.

If yours is to become an information-based organization then a change process needs to be designed. It will be necessary to start with an authentic picture of where you are so that people can acknowledge the present issues and those future dangerous opportunities. They can then develop a common vision as to where they wish to be and design a process to bridge between the present and the future. Set up pilot programmes to learn how to do this well, communicate and debate, and adapt behaviour and attitudes from these experiments. Encourage others to join in and create the corporate culture to reinforce these changes by consciously rewarding both financially and non-financially those moving in the right direction. It is most important for learning leaders to encourage feedback on a regular and rigorous basis to check that their mindsets and behaviours are in line with their espoused words and pictures of the future. People may be encouraged by politicians to 'watch my lips' but they always rate behaviour above the words spoken.

This sounds a simple process and in theory it is. But just as organizations could be quite comfortable places if there were no customers, so change would theoretically be easy if only there were no people involved. The tricky part of creating organizational change is the appropriateness and sensitivity of the process deployed. This determines the effectiveness of any change. This is why if directors are to become a true top team then they need to agree a common vision and values, accept and use their individual differences, and create feedback systems which give authentic information as to where they are, so that they can regularly monitor the change process, and so measure how far they have to go. The good news for directors is that the techniques for such top teambuilding are widely tested and easily available. The bad news is that they have seldom been applied, for the reasons given in Chapter 1. But matters are beginning to change and as the postwar generation of directors comes into power this process is likely to speed up.

Let us look at the nine-point process in more detail.

1. *Getting an Authentic Picture of the Present*

Getting people to come forward to talk about present problems and issues is not an easy task. It is much easier to talk of future possibilities because the results are more abstract, less personal and so more comfortable. Facing the hard facts about the present can be uncomfortable as there is an element of personal criticism within it. Each of us is part of the present situation and, if that has some problems in it, then we must be part of the cause. To derive authentic information we need to design a process by which we can all get into our helicopter and take an overview of the situation – without falling immediately into interpersonal fights about who is to blame. We need the skill to be able to distance ourselves from the problems to which we have contributed in part. To achieve this we need to create as risk-free an environment in which to take our soundings as possible. A promise, confirmed by later behaviour, that no Kafkaesque note will be made secretly on the personnel record of any participant will usually help to encourage the offering of constructive criticism.

There are many ways of handling the collection of such data. Perhaps the most effective, and certainly the most used as a starter process, is the SWOT (Strengths, Weaknesses, Opportunities and Threats) analysis. This looks at the present organization or department in terms of its strengths and weaknesses, and the future in terms of the environmental opportunities and threats. A SWOT quadrant is given to each participant in the information-gathering process for completion. Then they are brought together to debate their findings and their feelings about the present and the future. The process is often run by a skilled outsider so that the present power positions in the organization do not dominate what is being collected.

When the total inputs are agreed then a process of prioritizing the issues is undertaken on both the strengths and weaknesses and the opportunities and threats sides of the quadrant. An agreed SWOT map is drawn up with probabilities given to the opportunities and threats side. From this analysis organizational development needs can be deduced and suitable unblocking processes started both to free up the present and to allow achievement of the common vision of the future – which is what we want to flow from this.

Another useful tool in collecting authentic data about present and future aspirations is the *organizational climate survey*. Again, this is best undertaken by an outsider and, with responses kept confidential, it can derive useful data on the reality and the ideal positions for such dimensions as organizational clarity; responsibility; standards; conformity; leadership; financial rewards; non-financial rewards; and warmth and support. This can be so powerful a process that I have known clients refuse to release the final results 'in case they affect adversely our share price'. The resultant richness of information and ideas on to how to unblock the present reality can be worth its weight in gold – provided they are seen to be implemented and the respondents kept involved in the process. Without this then any survey can have negative effects as unreal aspirations are raised and then dashed by an uncomprehending top team.

The results from the SWOT or organizational climate analysis can be represented graphically by the use of a 'force field analysis' (see Figure 3.1). This maps the agreed opportunities and threats as opposing forces creating the present situation.

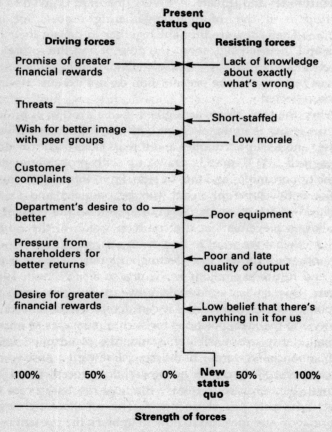

Figure 3.1   An example of the force field analysis[25]

Plotting the preferred situation on the chart allows for discussion and planning of the removal of some of the opposing forces, the threats. The argument is that the removal of even the more modest of the threats allows, with no extra energy from the opportunities side, the organization to grasp those very opportunities. Taking the opposite approach, as many directors do, of increasing the positive pressures rather than reducing the negative ones can have the perverse effect of increasing resistance.

2. *Developing a Common Vision*

Having a commonly agreed target greatly improves both the effectiveness and the efficiency of the organization. It is still remarkable how many organization surveys show little comprehension by employees of what the organization is actually trying to achieve, and how it will know when it has got there.

Developing a unifying common vision forms a powerful planning and emotionally committing source for the whole organization. It does not have to be a Panglossian view – of everything being for the best in the best of all possible worlds. There will be differences and the usual organizational micropolitics in all businesses. If the majority will commit themselves to a common vision of the future in which they have had a hand, then there is a good chance of creating sufficient organizational energy to achieve it. The psychological ownership of problems and opportunities is an evolving field of study. Research on influencing styles shows that many, but not all, top managers are comfortable creating common visions. The problem appears to be that they are often bad at communicating them. The very words and images used, as well as the style of the presentation, hinder the message and its acceptability. Research in the area of neuro-linguistic programming is showing some hopeful signs of how to get over this.

3. Design a Process for Bridging Between the Present and the Vision

This is the central responsibility of the top team. By this I do not mean to imply that they must therefore do it themselves. It is neither necessary nor wise for them to make the changes themselves; others can be given authority to do that. The learning leaders' role is to ensure that there is a system by which they can make progress and learn from it. Tapping the sources of problem-solving power in an organization, characterized by Revans[12] as:

- Who *knows* about the problem?
- Who *cares* about the problem?
- Who *can do* anything about the problem?

and bringing them into a 'temporary coalition of powers' can give a very good idea of what the design process needed to create the necessary changes might be.

4. Launching Pilot Programmes

Rather than try to solve all the problems identified by the surveying process at once it is usually wise to tackle a few of those which are seen as important and symbolic to achieving the total change needed. In this way solid success can be demonstrated and others then encouraged to tackle some of the more intractable problems. The number of pilot projects is immaterial. One success can transform an organization. But the size of any problem-solving pilot project is important – small to medium is a lot easier and faster to launch and learn from than are large and complex projects.

I try to derive some key experimental projects from the opportunities and threats side of the SWOT analysis. The essence is that they should be seen as 'crucial for our future survival'. I ask for the top team to identify what they see, individually, as those organizational issues which, unless resolved within say 18 months, will have sped the collapse of the organization. These are collected and discussed by the top team and then a final group of issues is selected as the basis of any pilot change programmes. Once agreed they ask for volunteers willing to develop themselves whilst developing their organization. Yes, *volunteers*. If one is to believe in 'taking responsibility for one's own development' then this is a powerful way to do it. The energy of committed enthusiasts, as individuals or groups, is of such richness that they will test the validity of any change process by doing their best to achieve the necessary changes and to feed back the learning.

Such people do exist, even in the most unlikely organizations. A recent experience in a local authority shows that even in what was characterized as a rather demoralized group of local government officials facing massive environmental changes the number of people wishing to put themselves forward to pull their organization out of its present trough was enormous. Some 30 action-learning groups put themselves up for pilot projects. In terms of the coalition of powers to create change they tended to come from the 'Who cares?' cateogry, i.e. those people in direct contact with the problem, even though they might not have the full information or power to create change. But that is what they have set out to learn about their organization.

The learning can be best diffused across the organization from the pilot projects by having each action-learning group formed from disciplines as mixed as possible. As previously mentioned in Chapter 2, such action-learning groups need the time and commitment to meet regularly (at least a day a fortnight), and to be able to criticize and support each other rigorously (by a 'set' of comrades in adversity). They need also delegated authority to take action on what they identify as organizational blockages in the system.

Without such delegated authority they will achieve an organizational version of analysis-paralysis and this will increase the frustration about the organization and its processes. The difference will be more powerful, as this time it is well informed. This delegation is an acid test of a director's ability to take his or her hands off the operations and let those who wish to develop themselves take over. Many participants think that even then they will not be able to create great changes in their organization. However, history shows us that a handful of committed people can make great changes. It is no coincidence that the English law of conspiracy starts with a minimum of three people.

5. *Communicate and Debate the Learning Achieved Openly*
The 'glasnost' approach to organizational learning is important to demonstrate the behaviours needed in learning leaders. There will be mistakes made and corporate myths shattered (as in Example 3.2). That is an essential part of the reframing process. It is much better to talk inside the organization of the successes achieved, and the things we would not do that way again, than to try and emulate Doctor Pangloss and try to prove that everything we do is always right for the best of all reasons. This means that we need to ensure that the action-

---

Example 3.2 Information, control and climate
The technical director of a major international company was horrified to find that the reality of their previous unsatisfactory position, and the energy of their current, hugely successful position, had been communicated by their senior management developers at a professional conference. Moreover, their paper was then published in a professional journal. He set out to discipline the developers and to threaten action against the journal because he thought it wrong that such information should be discussed as he thought it might upset the company's shareholders and customers. In the end the chief executive intervened and explained to the technical director that the new climate they were trying to encourage in the organization was one where authentic information flowed. This would mean that the customers and shareholders would also be better informed and that this, in turn, would create a healthy organizational climate. The technical director thought this a fundamental challenge to his authority because of the threat to his control of information. He has accepted reluctantly the chief executive's wishes but has made it clear that if he can change what is occurring, he will.

---

learning groups speak with each other, the line managers, the directors and the workforce, about what information was derived, what we did, what happened and what we have learned from it. This sets a style of communicating what is happening in real-time in the organization. This is often the most difficult thing for a director to contemplate, especially in times of rapid change. The old wail of footsoldiers – that all they do is 'hurry up and wait' without anyone ever explaining why – is reflected in most organizations. This part of the process helps get over that. It has another beneficial effect – it enthuses others to have a go and that is worth a lot more than all the usual investment in 'corporate communications'.

6. Encouraging Others to Join

This flows on from the above communication process. Once such an 'organizational transformation' is under way others will want to join for a mixture of reasons. Some will want to settle old scores, or ensure that the balance of micro-politics is returned so that they are not dominated by specific departments or individuals. Most join because they want to contribute their bit to the greater good of the organization. It is always pleasant to have to deal with a problem of success and that is what happens as others join in (Example 3.3). Rather than say 'no, we do not have any more resource' the creative learning leader will outline the resource issue and ask what they can do about it – a discriminating question. It is remarkable what

---

Example 3.3 Rubber workers commit to action learning
Whilst an action-learning programme was being instituted in a tyre factory to re-energize the middle and senior managers, the workforce was cynical over the help that could be given through the self-help 'sets'. After a couple of months, however, they started to copy, unofficially, the regular and rigorous set meetings to help solve their shopfloor problems. The senior managers quickly realized that this should be encouraged and, despite some initial union opposition, it has become the style for working and learning throughout the company.

---

ingenuity people will then show for their own and others' benefit. They generate many suggestions and the energy to deliver the results. The issue for top managers is how to feel comfortable with this amount of energy, and questioning, in the organization. It can seem daunting – one Japanese company reports that on average it implements over 5,000 staff suggestions per day. How many has your organization implemented in a year?

7. Creating the Reinforcing Corporate Culture

The crude definition of corporate culture is 'how we do things around here'. It will be seen that the action-learning approach to organizational development is a corporate culture in itself. However, it can be helpful to overlay this definition with a deeper analysis so that one can have some visible and agreed co-ordinates about which to debate the organizational culture. I have found Handy's *The Gods of Management*[26] helpful to directors in getting to grips with what might otherwise seem a very soft and academic topic.

In this book, Charles Handy builds on work which he and Roger Harrison have developed. He describes four main organizational cultures which, he argues, need careful identification before any organizational changes can be made to stick. He characterizes them as follows (but I must stress that the paraphrases are mine):

- The *power culture* – very much the one-man rule, or divide-and-rule, culture. Information is kept at the centre so that people operating on the spokes can be played off one against the other. Coalitions which challenge the centre are rapidly and ruthlessly put down. Such a culture tends towards win/lose fights and binary thinking. Little useful learning is possible for the majority but the folklore is rich in

 symbol:

examples of the charismatic eccentricities of the person at the centre.

- The *role culture* – essentially the bureaucratic model. Organizational procedures and values are highly codified and diffused. The people at the top are guardians of the status quo and tend to introversion and nit-picking. Everyone knows their place and there are tough sanctions should they step out of line. Making mistakes, or debating, is not encouraged and the folklore has horror stories about what happened to those who did.

symbol:

- The *task culture* – essentially a project-based model. Teams are brought together for periods of intense work, then disbanded. There is a lot of energy around and people are usually respected for their contributions – everyone is working to time and cost constraints and appreciates their role in the project. Organizationally it can seem messy and there are great fights over who has the 'ultimate' power over a specialist, the project manager or the head of the specialist function. Development can, therefore, be forgotten in the heady, action-based atmosphere unless ideas like 'centres of excellence' are introduced as counterweights.

symbol:

- The *people culture* – an apparently 'anarchic' model in organizational terms. It is without government in the sense that the people in it subscribe to highly specific and exclusive values. The focus is on each

symbol:

> person being treated equally, often as co-
> operators, with a say in objectives, product
> and process. Whilst great fun to be in at
> the start-up, people cultures tend to hit
> trouble when faced with decisions on
> resource allocation and, sadly, become
> battlegrounds for interpersonal fights.
> Then little learning is possible and they
> tend to die rapidly.

Such an analysis can often help clear the directors' thinking. There are few examples of such 'pure' cultures. Most of us live in organizations which espouse one set of values but behave according to another. The very complexity of overlying levels of micro-culture is why directors need to spend time in clarifying the issues without losing the valuable differences found there.

The question is 'What is my organization's dominant culture?' There will be different dominant cultures operating at different levels and within different departments of the organization. These can be found by surveying or by taking crude measures through asking some key questions of what it is like to be in the organization:

- What adjectives would you use to describe the organization now?
- How would you describe what you would like it to be in the future?
- What is the dominant management style?
- What is the dominant response style?
- Who gets which rewards and why?
- What happens when things go wrong?
- What creates most energy in the organization?

8. Rewarding Achievers and Triers

As participants in organizational development programmes become committed to the process it is necessary to institute reward systems that recognize those who achieve. Such rewards do not need to be simply financial. Extrinsic rewards – such as money, cars, stock options, etc – have a short-term energizing effect. In Herzberg's terms such 'hygiene factors' are necessary but not sufficient. Sufficiency comes from intrinsic factors such as recognition, the nature of the work itself, personal challenge, etc. These aspects of inclusion are essentially personal and self-motivating, although the conditions to create them can be managed by the learning leader.

This is not to suggest that directors need do nothing about people who are achieving their developmental aims because such achievement is reward enough. To return to my original definition of development, the second aspect is 'to make manifest' – this is the role for learning leaders. Part of the intrinsic reward itself is through recognition of both the public and the personal kind. The most effective form, and the least used by directors, is to say 'thanks' both face to face and through the organization's information systems. Sadly this is a little-practised leadership technique and its non-use can lead to unfortunate consequences. Studies on the human need for recognition show a variant on the law of human cussedness. A person seeks to be recognized as a natural need. If there is no recognition then they do not simply accept a lack of recognition over time. A person not recognized by someone in authority (be it director or parent) will say, 'Well if they will not give me any positive recognition for my contribution to this organization, then they will have to give me negative recognition.' They then do things which they know are wrong but which will at least get a response from those in authority. This can be by deliberately disobeying instructions or, more subtly, by malicious obedience to instructions known to be wrong. Human beings seek recognition to show that they are valued parts of the organization. It is the learning leader's role to ensure that this is positive recognition in line with the organization's objectives.

9. Getting Feedback on the Learning Leader's Behaviour

This is often the most powerful piece of learning for directors, and in the early days sometimes the most painful. It looks at the simple proposition that staff are likely to respond best to leaders whose words and actions are synchronized. This sounds deceptively easy. Sadly many directors tend to influence by relying on exhortation only. They expect people to do what they are told, often with little common vision or explanation. It is not then surprising if responses to these exhortations are diverse or even contradictory.

What is known is that the sensing systems of the people working in an organization are tuned to detect directoral doublespeak. Messages will flash across the organizational grapevine if the words and actions do not tally – thus proving it to be the most effective communications system of all. If 'they' say that we are cost-cutting across the organization, then have they given themselves large salary increases, or special dispensation to keep recruiting staff for their personal offices? If so, then people will not accept the exhortations, nor their leaders, as credible (see Example 3.4).

Example 3.4 Whitegoods quality
A consultant was brought in to help improve the quality of a whitegoods company. He analysed the problem and presented a solution to the top managers, who accepted it enthusiastically. A few weeks later the consultant, with the agreement of the managers, sat outside the company for a day and randomly stopped trucks to check on product quality. The results were not encouraging. Reporting back the top managers said, 'Yes, we had wanted to improve the quality but we were so very pushed for deliveries we had encouraged the staff to send out those that were near enough OK.' They did not see that this would affect their 'quality drive'.

A system needs to be installed where, during both the organizational development and the appraisal processes, the directors and managers are asking the same basic question of their staff, 'What can I do to make your work more effective?' Before macho managers blow a gasket, I should stress that this is not a soft option to get more resources to make life easier. It is rather an attitude of a learning leader willing to accept that they too might play a part in blocking the organization, and have a need to get feedback about what they can offer to unblock the situation. This 'Dynorod' school of leadership has much to recommend it because it keeps the directors in their proper orbit above the daily operational problems yet with the ability to reframe problems from a strategic viewpoint when necessary. It leaves authority with the line managers and staff to cope with their own deviations from the strategic plans.

Such a process also allows the board to have regular review meetings of their behaviours as reported by their people, and allows them to do what many boards yearn to be able to do – root firmly into the present truth about their organization rather than live in the judgemental past, or the visionary future. Creative ingenuity is often lacking in directors and top teams, so such feedback gives clues as to how the common visions might be reached, via the reality shown in the pilot projects. It helps bridge the gap between the difficult present and the future opportunities.

I realize that this organizational transformation process sounds simplistic. Linking present problems to future opportunities and threats via a system of organizational learning and the release of the problem-solving energies of the people who are the organization is easily said. I cannot make it specific to your organization to make it easy to achieve. But I can say that this approach seems to work and with only two conditions – that the leaders are seen to be committed to the change process, and that their words and actions are in synchronization.

4

Creating a Learning Climate in Our Organization

When Rhinoceroses Learn to Learn

By now, I trust I have demonstrated that organizations can learn to learn organically and systematically. I hope I have shown that learning is both necessary and sufficient for them to survive – the $L \geqslant C$ argument – and that in future the very learning itself will become a key tradable asset for the organization – its 'know how' and 'know why', or intellectual property.

Rosabeth Moss Kanter in her latest book named, significantly, *When Giants Learn to Dance*[27] points out that even the largest corporations, who until now had assumed that they determined markets and trends, are now having to face the environmental changes like anyone else. They are finding that sometimes their very size and inflexibility works against them in a time of rapid changes. The pressures on them now are to manage globally and yet continue to learn in this constantly changing and chaotic 'post-entrepreneurial' world. Here more traditional notions such as corporate discipline, focus, competitive edge and teamworking need to be married with entrepreneurial nimbleness and creativity. Kanter concludes her book by making the point that 'the post-entrepreneurial company represents a triumph of process over structure' – and this is the point I wish to develop in this chapter.

The Learning Organization

The most concise definition of the *learning organization* is 'an organisation which facilitates the learning of all its members and continuously transforms itself'.[28] You will notice that this definition is totally process-based – it rests firmly in the social–emotional area with none of the traditionally hard areas of management (structure, hierarchies, span of control, functional disciplines, etc) mentioned. One common fallacy attributed to the learning organization is that it is an organization that just does a lot of training. Not so. Nick Georgiades of British Airways has said:

> Training is a liability in situations where you have to flex quickly – what price the training you had yesterday because today I want you to do something different? ! But you will not do it because you are so wedded to what we trained you to do yesterday.

Paul Marsh of Jaguar expands the point on learning organizations:

> The first thought is that it's about a company, as a priority objective, developing all its human resources, enhancing all their skills . . . but not being content with that . . . learning from those people how the company can be improved . . . so that it becomes a cycle of learning.

Conditions for a Climate of Organizational Learning

I have listed below five conditions which are necessary for the free flow of learning and information so that an organization can continuously transform itself. These appear both necessary and sufficient but, as we are in the early days of research and development in this field of study, I am interested to hear of any refinements or amendments that readers have to offer. The five conditions show the state of my own thinking at present and I have said a little on each to show how the thinking evolved to this point.

1. A Perception of Learning as a Cyclical Process

I had decided that the cyclical nature of learning was important when I wrote *The Learning Organisation*[1] in 1987. Whilst the *policy/strategy/operations* hierarchy is useful in clarifying the director's role, it is a static concept. In a turbulent world this is of limited utility. It is true that one could add a flow of instructions running down the hierarchy, and a flow of feedback running back up it. I had to remember, however, the ancient tales of messengers who brought bad news being killed because of the content of the message. This is still part of organizational folklore and is the enemy of generating authentic information.

2. An Acceptance of the Different Roles of Policy, Strategy and Operations within the Organization

As I have argued this strongly throughout this book I will not over-egg the message save to say that understanding the rights and duties of each level of the organization, and then being comfortable in adapting one's role within the learning cycle to deal effectively with the information flows, is fundamental in creating a climate for organizational learning.

3. A Free Flow of Authentic Information

But the need for authentic feedback to create a true picture of the present reality, and to test the quality of strategic thought and planning, gave me a strong clue to a key condition for creating the climate of a learning organization. The need for continuous flows of non-corrupted or politicized information (rather than data) systems tends to sit uncomfortably with the reality of many organizations' management information systems. These tend to be concerned with neither management, information nor systems. True management information systems, i.e. those that give the directors and managers of an organization the ability to ask discriminating questions of the data produced from the MIS and get valid information from it, are central to the learning organization.

4. The Ability to Value People as the Key Asset for Organizational Learning

I have talked already about the cynicism that many staff have with regard to directors who say that 'people are our major asset'. They do not appear on the balance sheet, even now that intellectual property and brands are beginning to show up. Most directors' behaviour is in contradiction to the assertion. This is where nurturing, inclusion, coaching to competence and development come into their own. All of these need to be developed in learning leaders and then made manifest through attitudes and behaviours.

5. The Ability to Reframe Information at the Strategic Level: First and Second Order Change

Simultaneous with my interest in learning cycles and authentic information systems was an awareness of the helpful work of the 'brief therapists'[29] in the United States. They were arguing (in my crude characterization of their elegant work) that rather than invest a great deal of time and money in deep psychotherapy in the prone position so as to try to answer the question 'Why do I do this?', many people found it helpful to get quick and effective results by keeping people in the vertical plane and asking short, pragmatic, yet discriminating questions along the lines of 'How can we get you to take the first step in breaking out of the cycle in which you see yourself?' This is not to demean the deep therapists, rather to say that the options for clients were opened up. The brief therapists encouraged their clients to take the first step then and there, and to become aware of the cycle of thinking and behaviour which bound their people.

This assumed that the environment, the contexts, in which they found themselves were given, so there was little they could do about them. All they felt that could be done was 'more of . . .' or 'less of . . .' what was already happening. The parallels with the operations cycle of an organization struck me forcibly. This convergent view of the world was known as 'first order change'. It had a tinge of desperation about it, particularly if one was aware of the change around one but felt there was little one could do to change it – a very common human view. But some people broke out of this cycle and in so doing were able to reframe their perspective – to get above the problem and cast different lights and views upon it. This ability to create a helicopter view was known as 'second order change'.

Integrating the Five Conditions into the Learning Organization

The idea of first and second order change, and the need for leaders to have the ability to change perspectives, interested me greatly. It fitted well with work that Tony Hodgson[30] and I had developed in the early 1980s. We linked the policy, strategy and operations hierarchy into the idea of learning cycles. Later I added the brief therapists' ideas and found a distinct model appearing (see Figure 4.1).

At the operations level the cycle, and mindset, are essentially of first order change – people tend to be so busy and head down in the work that their responses to problems tend towards action fixation and doing 'more of . . .' or 'less of . . .'

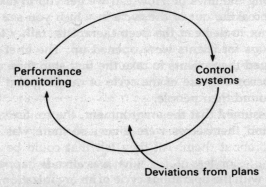

Figure 4.1 The operational cycle of organizational learning

what is already happening. This is particularly true at present when targets and budgets have been tightened. Time is then spent by the majority of the organization designing and tightening operational control systems to try and keep out any moves away from agreed plans.

Performance is monitored against plans and appropriate action taken through the control systems. Ideally the whole is run like a well-oiled machine – were it not for the deviations from plans which break into the operations rhythm like a Monty Python foot from the sky. It is managing these deviations back on to plan that gives many people meaning in their organizational life. Once a deviation is apparent, people rush about saying 'the sky is falling', we must do more of this and less of that. This need for drama is found in all cultures. Research shows that some, especially the British, Irish, Swedish and Danes, tend to build it in if it does not exist.

The *second order change* cycle of learning seemed to fit with the policy formulation level of the hierarchy. It is at this interface with the changing external world that the reframing process is able to occur. Here one rises above the day-to-day routines of managing the operational deviations from plans. This process of monitoring the external environment, giving thoughtful leadership and direction, and formulating policy is the natural habitat of directors. (Another Pythonesque foot crashes out of the sky into this strategic learning cycle through disruptions from the environment.) Here there is little chance that an organization could directly influence such disruptions – be they oil price rises or drops, or a *coup d'état* in the state of a key client. This is what makes it so frustrating for many aspiring directors, and why so many do not bother to master it. Coping with, and using to advantage, the turbulent environment is a necessary and developable skill (see Figure 4.2).

A scientific explanation of 'turbulence' states,

it is a mess of disorder at all scales, small eddies within larger

109

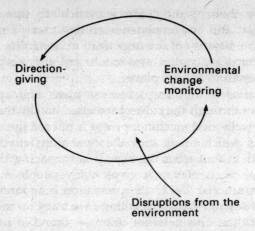

Direction-giving

Environmental change monitoring

Disruptions from the environment

Figure 4.2   The policy cycle of organizational learning

ones. It is unstable. It is highly dissipative, meaning that turbulence drains energy and creates drag. It is motion turned random.[19]

This feeling of Brownian motion is an enlightening metaphor to describe the thoughts and feelings of directors towards their external environment. Whilst directors' psychological profiles usually show a high need to be in control (and not be controlled by others) the reality in a turbulent environment is that they are not. This they do not like and, consequently, they often avoid either monitoring the changes or take perverse pleasure in 'shooting' the messengers who bring them bad news from the environment. Neither is a useful activity except to give vent to some minor sadism – as many group planning departments, corporate economists and politicians know, having been on the receiving end of frustrated directors.

That monitoring the external environment is necessary is not disputed by directors. But most are troubled by the feeling of incompetence that having to do so creates within them. The intellectual processes of coping with ambiguity and uncertainty, then learning to value and finally to use the energies created by them – the 'judo approach' to strategy – are developable. But my experience shows that they are only effective if undertaken as a top team process. That is, those directing the organization need to take seriously both their self-development and their top team development before they can assume the role of learning leaders in a learning organization.

I had noted that many directors failed to become learning leaders because of their unhappiness at spending a significant amount of their time 'brain on' rather than 'hands on'. For them such a leadership style was uncomfortable, so their direction-giving capacities were often diverted back into operations instead. This led to the previously mentioned organizational issues of 'Who gives the directions?' and 'How do we unblock the development of those squashed by directors returning to the comfort of their old functional jobs?' What could be done to help?

Integrating the Learning Cycles Through Strategy
Organizational life is not as simple as having two distinct binary cycles of learning with which to deal. They need integration and, as Rosabeth Moss Kanter has stated,[27] in process rather than structural terms. The obvious way of integrating them was by creating three cycles of learning with a key central one, *strategy*, that constantly processed the other two and, by so doing, reframed each. The changes in the external world could be fed through to operations, and the realities of what operations could deliver at any one time would allow better information as to how to deploy the organization's scarce resources in the changing environment and so create more thoughtful plans, and a more responsive organization.

Learning leaders sit at the centre of such a strategic organizational learning process. They become the 'business brain' of their organization – the focus of the learning of their enterprise and its corporate memory. There is a need to break out of the Bourbon thinking of unlearning organizations – their inbuilt ability to learn nothing and forget nothing. It is the directors' role to ensure, via the corporate memory, that learning is possible. They do not do all the learning themselves; indeed they cannot. But they can create conditions under which the people who comprise the organization can learn how to learn whilst working, and then continue to learn as part of the organization's development system. This is the central process of organizational learning and the learning leaders are the central processors (Figure 4.3).

The Role of the Directors as Learning Leaders in the Learning Organization

Learning leaders need to be located centrally in the learning process. Learning does not naturally flow to the top of the organization. If directors are to grow healthy and effective organizations, then they need to accept that they are not the only people allowed to learn in the organization. People are learning, or having their learning blocked, all the time. It is by creating the conditions to encourage such learning, and then being seen to value it, that this fundamental role of directing is developed.

Learning is a human drama. It is worth remembering that when the word 'entrepreneur' came into the English language its present financial orientation was only secondary to that of the impresario – 'the stager of dramas'. This is a helpful metaphor for the learning leader – taking the crucial organizational issues and creating dramas by which they and their staff can learn how to become more effective.

A wise old company chairman heard me talking about this. He stayed behind after my presentation whilst we went to lunch. When I returned he had relabelled my three cycles of learning. He had labelled them his 'Directors' Manifesto' (Figure 4.4).

This may be a useful point for me to stop talking about the learning organization and encourage you to experiment with

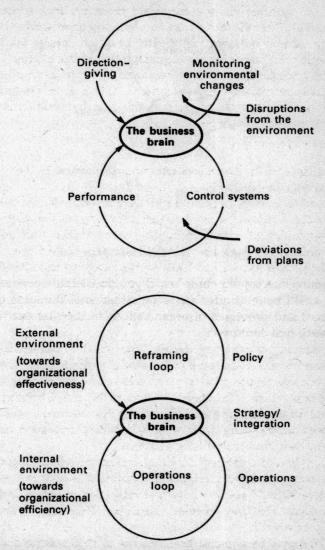

Figure 4.3   The learning organization and the three-level hierarchy

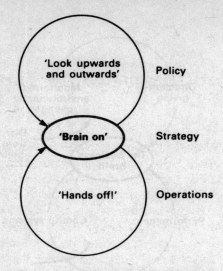

Figure 4.4   The Directors' Manifesto

it yourself. A lot of people are. If you do wish to keep reading, then all I have to offer are some rather brief thoughts on the nature and processes of organizations in the first part of the twenty-first century.

5

A Brief Glimpse of the Future

Like everybody else I cannot predict the future. If I could, life would be infinitely easier and much more boring. However, I, like everyone else, can scan the environment and watch for curious and unusual trends and blips to see if they are portents of much bigger changes about which we need to think if we are to survive and develop. Donald Schon in *Beyond the Stable State*[31] says that all major changes start at the periphery and move towards the centre. It is those changes for which we are looking.

We have already mentioned the work of Drucker, Handy and Kanter. Their ideas on *new order* organizations revolve around information-based, educated and nimble organizations all geared to cope with continuous change and development. My own work on the learning organization seems to have struck a sympathetic chord with directors in Europe and the Far East as it tries to synthesize both the content and the processes needed to cope with this increasingly dynamic environment. These look likely to be the basis of strategic management thought into the early years of the twenty-first century.

I would like to conclude this book by looking at developing ideas in the field of 'reframing', which has formed one of the sub-plots throughout this book. In structural terms one can see a sequential movement in mindsets of organizational form from the basic pyramid, through the inverted pyramid of the 'customer-service' organization, to the information technology-driven 'arrow head' organization, to the dynamic cycles of the 'learning organization' (see Figure 5.1).

Other reframing ideas are developing at the periphery which

A brief glimpse of the future

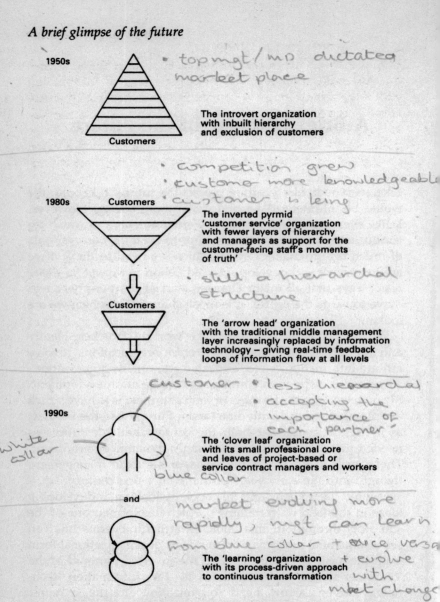

1950s

Handwritten: • top mgt/MD dictated market place

The introvert organization
with inbuilt hierarchy
and exclusion of customers

Customers

Handwritten: • competition grew
• customer more knowledgeable
• customer is king

1980s Customers

The inverted pyrmid
'customer service' organization
with fewer layers of hierarchy
and managers as support for the
customer-facing staff's moments
of truth'

Handwritten: • still a hierarchal structure

Customers

The 'arrow head' organization
with the traditional middle management
layer increasingly replaced by information
technology – giving real-time feedback
loops of information flow at all levels

Handwritten: customer • less hierarchal
• accepting the importance of each 'partner'

1990s

Handwritten: white collar

The 'clover leaf' organization
with its small professional core
and leaves of project-based or
service contract managers and workers

Handwritten: blue collar

and

Handwritten: market evolving more rapidly, mgt can learn in from blue collar + vice versa + evolve with mkt change

The 'learning' organization
with its process-driven approach
to continuous transformation

Figure 5.1 The sequence of mindsets symbolizing organizational form

116

Handwritten: L ≥ C

I think are well worth consideration. First, Max Boisot's work on the codification and diffusion processes of information within an organization – described in *Information and Organizations*[32] – suggests that information itself will become the key energy source of the twenty-first-century organization. In so doing it will challenge the basis of economics, which has relied on the notion of land, labour and capital being the key economic variables.

Moreover, Boisot's work has argued that the positioning of the functional departments of an organization are key to its ability to learn effectively. Each has a strategic place in the learning cycle, so any mis-positioning, or blockage, reduces the effectiveness of organizational learning. Central to the control of this process is the strategic positioning of the directors – in his terms the general management (see Figure 5.2).

This idea of 'directors as conductors', also mentioned by

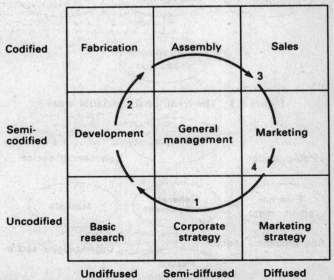

Figure 5.2 Specialist department positioning on Boisot's learning cycle

Peter Drucker, is reflected in an article by Professor John Morris.[33] He sees a four-stage reframing process which moves from the traditional specialist areas (Figure 5.3) through more of a helicopter view which transcends those traditional views and brings into perspective the sectors which need to be co-ordinated by the general managers (Figure 5.4). This continues through a more strategic view of the power groupings in and around the organization (Figure 5.5) to a final view of the *strategic qualities* which directors need to question and develop for the future (Figure 5.6).

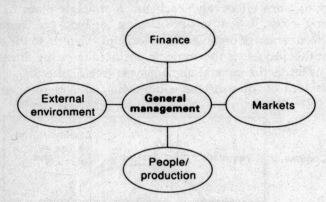

Figure 5.3   The traditional specialist areas

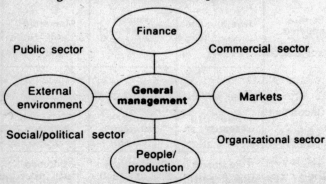

Figure 5.4   A transcending view of the traditional areas

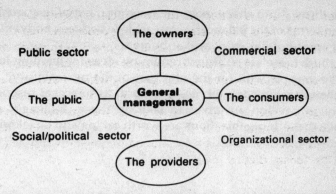

Figure 5.5 The strategic management of power groupings

Figure 5.6 The strategic future? Balancing the organizational qualities for competitiveness

This latter illustration is the real challenge for learning leaders. It throws up issues about power in organizations which will become increasingly important as we have to mean it when we say 'people are our chief asset'. It throws up questions about our organization's relationship to customer service and the total quality of our products and services. It throws up the increasingly important issue of the relationship between our organization and the physical environment. It also throws into sharp relief the issue of the *quality of working life* in terms of the balance we can achieve between body, mind and spirit both at work and at home.

I think these are sufficient reframing ideas for learning leaders to grapple with for the first part of the next century. The challenge is already with us. It is up to us to accept responsibility to develop ourselves to take up these challenges and prove that our organizations are worth saving and developing.

References

Although not referred to directly in the text I must acknowledge my debt to *The Colours of Your Mind* by Jerry Rhodes and Sue Thame (Collins, London, 1988), which suffuses much of my thinking about the development of learning leaders.

1. Garratt, Bob, *The Learning Organization* (Fontana, London, 1987).

2. Peter, Lawrence, *The Peter Principle* (Pan Books, London, 1989).

3. Redding, S. Gordon, 'Culture gap', *Asia Business & Industry*, April 1978, pp. 45–50.

4. Smith, Peter, 'The stages in a manager's job', in *Current Research in Management*, Hammond, Valerie (ed.) (Frances Pinter Publishers, London, 1986).

5. Mant, A., *The Leaders We Deserve* (Martin Robertson, Oxford, 1983).

6. Chen, A. & C. (trans.) *The Art of War* (Graham Brash Publishers, Singapore, 1982).

7. Honey, Peter and Mumford, Alan, *The Manual of Learning Styles* (Ardingly House, 10 Linden Avenue, Maidenhead, Berkshire SL6 6H, 1982).

8. Ashby, W. R., 'Self regulation and requisite variety', in *Introduction to Cybernetics* (Wiley, London, 1956).

9. Argenti, John, *Corporate Collapse: Causes and Symptoms* (McGraw-Hill, New York, 1976).

10. Hersey, Paul and Blanchard, Kenneth, *Management of Organizational Behaviour: Utilizing Human Resources* (Prentice-Hall, Englewood Cliffs, New Jersey, 1982). LEAD can be obtained from University Associates International,

Challenge House, 45–7 Victoria Street, Mansfield, Nottinghamshire NG18 5SU.

11. Dixon, Michael, 'The laws of organizational stupidity', *Financial Times*, 14 June 1989, p. 19.

12. Revans, R., *The Origins of Action Learning* (Chartwell-Bratt, Bromley and Lund, 1982).

13. Handy, Charles, *The Making of Managers* (MSC/NEDO/BIM, HMSO, London, 1987).

14. Constable, John and McCormick, Roger, *The Making of British Managers* (BIM/CBI, London, 1987).

15. Consultative Document on the Proposed National Framework for Management Development (CMED, London, 1988).

16. *Management Challenge for the 1990s* (The Training Agency, Sheffield, 1989).

17. Blanchard, Kenneth and Johnson, Spencer, *The One Minute Manager* (William Morrow, New York, 1982).

18. Japanese Productivity Council via the OECD Report 'The emerging attitudes and motivations of workers' (Paris, 1971).

19. Gleick, James, *Chaos* (Cardinal, Sphere, London, 1988).

20. Postle, Denis, *Catastrophe Theory* (Fontana, London, 1980).

21. Kuhn, Thomas, *The Structure of Scientific Revolutions* (University of Chicago Press, Chicago, 1962).

22. Chambers, C., Coopey, J. and Maclean, A., *Develop Your Management Potential* (Kogan Page, London, 1990).

23. Drucker, Peter F., 'The coming of the new organization', *Harvard Business Review*, January–February 1988.

24. Handy, Charles, *The Age of Unreason* (Basic Books, London, 1989).

25. Plant, Roger, *Managing Change and Making It Stick* (Fontana, London, 1987).

26. Handy, Charles, *The Gods of Management* (Pan, London, 1985).

27. Kanter, Rosabeth Moss, *When Giants Learn to Dance* (Simon and Schuster, New York, 1989).

28. Pedler, Mike, Boydell, Tom and Burgoyne, John, 'Towards the learning company', *Management Education and Development*, vol. 20, part 1, Spring 1989.

29. Watzlawick, P., Weakland, J. and Fisch, R., *Change: Problem Formulation and Problem Resolution* (W. W. Norton and Company, New York, 1974).

30. Hodgson, Tony, *Communikit* (High Trenhouse, Malham Moor, Settle, North Yorkshire BD24 9PR).

31. Schon, Donald, *Beyond the Stable State* (Penguin, Harmondsworth, 1967).

32. Boisot, Max, *Information and Organizations: The Manager as Anthropologist* (Fontana, London, 1987).

33. Morris, John, 'Good company', *Management Education and Development*, vol. 18, part 2, pp. 103–15, 1987.

Index

Walstam, Gunnar, x
Watzlawick, Weakland and
   Fisch, x
Weber, Max, 87

Welch, Barry, xi
Wilkinson, Dave, xi
'Winter of Discontent', the, 82

What is AMED?

AMED is an association of individuals who have a professional interest in the development of people at work. Our membership is exclusive to individuals. AMED's network brings together people from industry, the public sector, academic organizations and consultancy.

The aims of the association

- to promote best practice in the fields of individual and organizational development

- to provide a forum for exploration of new ideas

- to provide our members with opportunities for their own development

- to encourage the adoption of ethical practices

Benefits of membership

- an extensive network of contacts

- regional groups spanning the UK and Europe

- shared experience of working on leading-edge issues

- local meetings and special interest networking activities

- a programme of national conferences, workshops and seminars

- a regular AMED newsletter and a quarterly journal

- a membership list and consultants' directory

- discounts on publications and professional insurances

- a national voice on development issues

Registered office:
Association for Management Education & Development
14–15 Belgrave Square
London SW1X 8PS
Tel: 071 235 3505
Fax: 071 235 3565   Registered Charity No 269 706

The Learning Organization

Bob Garratt

The Successful Strategist series
Edited by Bob Garratt

Practical and provocative, this book by one of the world experts in management education offers a fresh perspective on the way organizations work.

Bob Garratt proposes a theory of organizations as 'learning systems' in which success depends on the ability of managers to become 'direction-givers' and on the organization's capacity for learning continuously. As well as considering the work of other business thinkers, Garratt employs a wide range of experimental models and graphic illustrations to demonstrate both the stagnation which results from the absence of these skills, and the dramatic effects of their positive implementation.

Fully updated to take into account the new business conditions of the 1990s, *The Learning Organization* is a seminal work, exciting, informative and a challenge to all directors, management educators and the business community at large.

'This book is needed, and has stimulated my thoughts. I welcome its publication'　　　　　　　　　　　　　　　Sir Adrian Cadbury

'I read it with great interest and profit'　　　Professor Charles Handy

ISBN 0 00 638325 4

Information and Organizations
The Manager as Anthropologist

Max Boisot

The Successful Strategist series
Edited by Bob Garratt

Information and Organizations develops a radically new approach to organizations within the field of business management. In recent years the obvious failure of conventional management techniques to solve our industrial ills has given rise to a new concept of 'organization culture'. However, this is a term easier to label than define, and in this book Max Boisot demonstrates that organization culture is better understood when examined using some of the tools of the anthropologist.

He discusses how the related concepts of information sharing and information structuring combine to produce communication strategies that express different attitudes to authority, knowledge and business relationships. He goes on to explain how these concepts operate in a firm as it develops from a small domestic base to a large multinational corporation. Drawing on his field experience in Asia, Max Boisot also looks at the Japanese corporation and explores the culture problems faced by Chinese enterprises under Deng Xiaoping's reforms.

'Shows an enormous breadth of technical knowledge and should find a place on the shelf of any student of management'
Sir David Plastow, MD and Chief Executive, Vickers PLC

ISBN 0 00 637126 4

Manage Your Time

Sally Garratt

The Successful Manager series
Edited by Bob Garratt

'The working day just isn't long enough . . . I never have enough time'

This, the distress call of so many managers, is something that can be cured. Solving your time management problems will not only make you more efficient day to day, but it will enable you to plan more effectively for your company's future, and spend more time enjoying your personal life.

Sounds impossible? Sally Garratt, who has run numerous personal-effectiveness courses for managers, shows that it can be done. She examines every area of time management – from the telephone and the 'open door', to the diary and setting priorities. She looks at how you cope with meetings, organize your office, the way you plan ahead and how you give work to your staff (if you give work to your staff!) There is an invaluable section on delegation, with advice on when you should and when you shouldn't delegate.

Practical, realistic, and packed with real-life examples, this book will open the door to more effective management of your time.

'It reminds managers of the things they know they should be doing and rarely do. I recommend it for all managers'
Michael Bett, President, Institute of Personnel Management

ISBN 0 00 638411 0

Managing Yourself

Mike Pedler and Tom Boydell

How well do you manage yourself?
Are you in control of your ideas, feelings and actions?
Does your life have purpose and direction?
Have you enough personal energy?

Anyone who wants to improve the way they manage others must first learn to manage themselves. Starting from the inside out, managers need to become more aware of what they are doing in the areas of:

- health – physical, mental and emotional
- skills – social and technical
- action – how you get things done
- identity – valuing and being yourself

This practical guide for the 'thinking manager' contains case studies and useful activities to undertake which are designed to help you increase your effectiveness in managing yourself and your life and in improving your performance both at work and elsewhere.

Published in cooperation with The Association for Management Education and Development.

ISBN 0 00 636892 1

Titles in the *Successful Manager* series

All these books are available from your local bookseller or can be ordered direct from the publishers.

To order direct just tick the titles you want and fill in the form below:

Name: _____

Address: _____

_____

Postcode: _____

Send to: HarperCollins Mail Order, Dept 8, HarperCollins*Publishers*, Westerhill Road, Bishopbriggs, Glasgow G64 2QT.

Please enclose a cheque or postal order or your authority to debit your Visa/Access account –

Credit card no: _____

Expiry date: _____

Signature: _____

– to the value of the cover price plus:

UK & BFPO: Add £1.00 for the first and 25p for each additional book ordered.

Overseas orders including Eire, please add £2.95 service charge.

Books will be sent by surface mail but quotes for airmail despatches will be given on request.

24 HOUR TELEPHONE ORDERING SERVICE FOR ACCESS/VISA CARDHOLDERS –

TEL: GLASGOW 041-772 2281 or LONDON 081-307 4052